Sarah Ludwig

EPSOM DOWNS

Commissioned and first performed by the Joint Stock Theatre
Company in August 1977, Howard Brenton's *Epsom Downs*
takes place on Derby Day in Silver Jubilee Year. In the words
of *The Times* critic, Irving Wardle, the play explores 'a great
public festival, held on common land and pulling in punters of
every degree from the Aga Khan to the homeless family who
are camping out in a Dormobile. Half a dozen threads of plot
are woven in and out of a teeming Brueghel-like composition,
vying with jubilee chicken and Kermit Frog salesmen and other
genre detail, warring bookies and allegorical figures speaking for
Epsom itself.' All in all, *Epsom Downs* is 'a marvel of expressive
economy'.

'Brenton's portrait of Derby Day is, like Jonson's play
(Bartholomew Fair), an exuberant documentary about a secular
English festival. . . the result is his most accessible and simply
enjoyable play.'

Michael Billington, *The Guardian*

'Brenton's writing is rippling with comic observation and moves
with the tough confidence of someone who knows how to tell a
funny story. . . He has written a kaleidoscopic sequence which
manages to be both entertainment and shrewd social comment.'

John Peter, *The Sunday Times*

'Brenton's writing has never been so accessible and
compassionate. . .'

Ann McFerran, *Time Out*

*The photo on the front cover shows Will Knightley as a Derby
jockey and Tony Rohr as his horse in the Joint Stock production.
It is reproduced by courtesy of John Haynes. The photograph
on the back cover is reproduced by courtesy of Snoo Wilson.*

Howard Brenton

EPSOM DOWNS

On Epsom Downs I met my love
An iron fist in a satin glove

METHUEN · LONDON

A METHUEN PAPERBACK

First published in 1977 by Eyre Methuen Ltd,
11 New Fetter Lane, London EC4P 4EE
Reprinted 1982, 1983 by Methuen London Ltd
Copyright © 1977 by Howard Brenton
ISBN 0 413 38940 5 (Hardback)
ISBN 0 413 38930 8 (Paperback)

CAUTION
All rights whatsoever in this play are strictly reserved and
application for performance etc, should be made before
rehearsal to Margaret Ramsay Limited of 14a Goodwin's Court,
St. Martin's Lane, London, WC2N 4LL. No performances may be
given unless a licence has been obtained.

Printed in Great Britain by
Richard Clay (The Chaucer Press) Ltd,
Bungay, Suffolk

Set IBM by ⫪ Tek-Art, Croydon, Surrey

To Harry

Author's Note

JOINT STOCK has a distinctive way of working with a play-
wright. The final text is the writer's alone, but it is written in
full view of the company's constant, questioning gaze. I am
indebted to them for their painstaking research, their
encouragement and stamina, their endless but always creative
criticism, their flair and invention in workshops and rehearsals,
and for the many happy hours we spent together on race-courses
during the flat-racing season of 1977.

Howard Brenton

Characters

BOBBY, seven years old
PRIMROSE, a traveller
SANDY, a father
CHARLES PEARCE, a horse
  trainer
SUPERINTENDENT BLUE
SAWBONES, a horse
POLICE HORSE
KERMIT FROG TRADER
MARGARET, a mother
SHARON, three years old
MAN DOWN ON HIS LUCK
LORD RACK, a racing man
HUGH, a stable lad
JOCKS, a stable lad
MINTY, a traveller
MR TILLOTSON, an
  evangelist
MISS MOTROM, an
  evangelist
MACK, a busker
BUD, a busker
GRANDPA
GHOST, of Emily Davison
BUNNY GIRL
DOROTHY DELAUNE, a
  society woman

ROGER COYLE, a society
  man
THE AGA KHAN
AGA KHAN'S BODYGUARD
LES BACKSHAKER, a
  bookmaker
MORRY BURROWS, a
  bookmaker
MRS BACKSHAKER
JUBILEE CHICKEN VENDOR
LOUIS, a bookmaker
JUBILEE DRUNK
POLICEMAN
STABLE LAD
HORSE, running in The Derby
FOUR OWNERS
JOCKEY
WOMAN, at the beer tent
1ST BEER TENT DRUNK
2ND BEER TENT DRUNK
THE DERBY
THE COURSE
Lester Piggot fans, drunks,
  crowds, jockeys, lovers,
  asylum inmates

EPSOM DOWNS was commissioned and first performed by the Joint Stock Theatre Company at the Round House, Chalk Farm, London on 8 August 1977. The cast was as follows:

Gillian Barge	MISS MOTROM SHARON HORSE OWNER WOMAN AT THE BEER TENT
Simon Callow	SANDY THE AGA KHAN LES BACKSHAKER HORSE OWNER BEER TENT DRUNK
Paul Freeman	LORD RACK ROGER COYLE JUBILEE DRUNK STABLE LAD SAWBONES BUD
Tony Rohr	CHARLES PEARCE MACK MORRY HORSE RUNNING IN THE DERBY THE COURSE
Bob Hamilton	SUPERINTENDENT BLUE MAN DOWN ON HIS LUCK GRANDPA LOUIS BEER TENT DRUNK
Cecily Hobbs	MARGARET MINTY BUNNY GIRL HORSE OWNER
Will Knightley	MR TILLOTSON HUGH JOCKEY POLICEMAN KERMIT FROG TRADER

David Rintoul	BOBBY POLICE HORSE JOCKS JUBILEE CHICKEN TRADER THE DERBY
Jane Wood	PRIMROSE GHOST DOROTHY DELAUNE
All the cast also played:	LESTER PIGGOT FANS, DRUNKS, CROWDS, JOCKEYS, LOVERS, ASYLUM INMATES.

Directed by Max Stafford-Clark
Designed by Peter Hartwell
Lighting by Gareth Jones
Company and Stage Manager Alison Ritchie
Deputy Stage Manager Donna Rolfe
Assistant Stage Manager Alastair Palmer

Act One

BOBBY, *a seven year old, runs over the Downs flying a kite. He wears an indian headress of plastic feathers and has a plastic space-ray machine-gun hung on his back. BOBBY goes off. The kite remains in the sky.*

The Downs deserted.

PRIMROSE *a traveller, aged fifteen, comes on. She is dressed in a floral skirt, day-glow bright blue slacks beneath, a white blouse and a small frilly apron. She carries a basket full of twigs of heather and pieces of silver-paper. She also holds a David Soul magazine. She sits down on the slope of the hill. She lies back, sunbathing, the magazine over her face.*

The Downs, PRIMROSE sunbathing, the kite above.

SANDY, *aged thirty-four, with long hair on a receding pate, comes on dribbling a football. He has a cigarette in his mouth and carries an opened can of lager. He performs a few tricks with the ball. He stops, out of breath. He stretches his arms above his head. He attempts a press-up with the cigarette in his mouth. He gives up. He looks up into the sky. He whistles like a lark. He shades his eyes, squinting. He shrugs. He stands messily. He dribbles the ball off, over the skyline.*

The Downs, still. PRIMROSE sunbathing. Above, the kite flutters.

SUPERINTENDENT BLUE *and* CHARLES PEARCE *appear on the skyline, on horseback. The horses are played by naked actors.*

PEARCE. A lark. Up by that kite.

    PEARCE *and* BLUE *look up whistling.*

BLUE. The great day. It looks beautiful, does it not?

PEARCE. What?

BLUE. The South of England on the great day. Like a fat mattress on a fat bed.

    PEARCE *snorts.*

PEARCE. A bed soon to be trampled on by the common herd.

BLUE. It will be a very tough day. But we do love it so, do we not?

PEARCE. Do we?

PEARCE's horse starts.

Don't you, Mr. Bones.

BLUE. Good God, that Sawbones?

PEARCE. Blaze like a sickle. It is he.

BLUE. Your first first-class winner.

PEARCE. And you still smell it, don't you old man. The whiff of a great racecourse. The ozone of a   competitive life. Probably fear.

PEARCE pats the HORSE.

Failed at stud though, didn't you. Silly old bugger. So I hack him for the memory.

BLUE. Sentimental of you, Charles.

PEARCE. The racing world is full of sentimental pigs. Sitting on horses.

They laugh.

BLUE. Derby Day. The Cockney's holiday. Half a million cheeky chappies on the grass stuffing 'emselves with Brown Ale and ham sandwiches. It has a lot of old world charm.

PEARCE. Always makes me shudder. When you look at half a million punters laid out on a hill — you think 'Democracy could go mad'.

BLUE. Never.

PEARCE. I'm glad the crowd control overlord is calm.

BLUE. I am shitting hot bricks. But that is my job.

PEARCE. That is your job.

BLUE. No no, come on. We are both Epsom boys. And both come far. You a trainer of two runners in the Derby, Charles?

PEARCE. And you the trainer of the Derby crowd, Alan?

BLUE. On horses since we were children, school satchels on our backs.

PEARCE. Now on horses with ulcers in our stomachs.

BLUE. There is a pride, Charles. Local boys made good.

PEARCE. Yes, I give you that. There is a pride. Funny to
think — I have done business with the Queen Mother.

BLUE. There is a lot to be said for a Grammar School education.

PEARCE. We have come far. But I sometimes think we could
find ourselves going all the way back again. I think that when
I see a crowd.

BLUE. The Derby crowd is the fruit displayed. The odd rotten
pineapple, but that is all.

A TRADER *appears carrying a big bundle of violent green
soft toys, 'Kermit Frogs'. They are large — about three feet
long.* PEARCE *and* BLUE *eye the* TRADER.

Morning.

TRADER. Morning.

BLUE. Frogs?

TRADER. Right first time.

BLUE. Will mankind buy anything?

TRADER. Right again.

BLUE. They did not hop off a lorry, did they? Those frogs?
Onto your honest shoulder?

TRADER. Me, the wife and kids — have been slaving over these
frogs since Easter, to flog to the punters today.

BLUE. How very moving.

TRADER. What, want to see my licence to trade?

BLUE. Too early in the morning, Lad.

TRADER. Right.

THE TRADER, *going. He turns back.*

You Mr Pearce? The Trainer? I follow your horses.

PEARCE. I am charmed.

TRADER. Not today though.

PEARCE. I am uncharmed.

TRADER. What do you think of the Groom?

PEARCE. French brothel-creeper of an animal.

TRADER. Won't stay?

PEARCE. Let me put it like this. If Blushing Groom wins The Derby today, I will eat the Pope.

TRADER. Oh. And I was going to put my frogs on it. Took it as a sign. French horse? Frogs? No?

PEARCE. No.

TRADER. No. Nice talking to you. Hope we all have a good day. All in the same boat, are we not?

BLUE. You reckon?

TRADER. Service industries to the mugs upon the Downs. The horseflesh, the law and order, the Kermit Frogs.

BLUE. Don't be fresh.

TRADER. Let's hope we all clean up, anyway.

The TRADER *goes off over the skyline.*

PEARCE. Phew.

BLUE. Phew.

PEARCE. All kinds.

BLUE. Well. Better get back. Bite a few necks.

PEARCE. Me too.

They walk their horses.

BLUE. If Blushing Groom blows up, what do you fancy? Piggot?

PEARCE. If Lester Piggott wins The Derby today, I will marry the Pope. Race you?

BLUE. To the Gyppo Evangelical tent?

PEARCE. You're on. Hup!

BLUE. Hup!

They gallop their horses off. The Downs deserted. The kite flutters above.

MARGARET *pushes* SHARON, *aged three years, over the grass in a baby buggy.*

SHARON. My want a ginger biscuit.

MARGARET *zigzags down the slope with the baby buggy.*

SHARON. My want a ginger biscuit.

MARGARET. You cannot have a ginger biscuit. You have just had your porridge. Let's go fast and fly! Right up to the kite!

SHARON. My not want to fly — up the kite — my want a ginger biscuit!

MARGARET. You cannot have a ginger biscuit. You have just had your porridge.

SHARON. My want to see the horses.

MARGARET. You will see horses later.

SHARON. My want to see horses now!

MARGARET. Oh God, I have given birth to a female Ghengis Khan. It is early in the morning now, sweetheart. You have just got us all up, sweetheart. You'll see the horses later. Look at the kite. It's like a bird.

SHARON. NOT like a bird. My NOT look at the kite. MY want a ginger biscuit.

MARGARET. You cannot have a ginger biscuit. You have just had your porridge — come on, let's go fast —

She runs the baby buggy in a figure eight.

SHARON. WHY MY just had my porridge?

MARGARET. Don't be a little bugger or I'll tickle you.

SHARON. MY WANT — set that kite on fire.

MARGARET *stops and tickles* SHARON.

No no! NOT tickle me! NOT.

SHARON *yells but ends up giggling.*

NOT do that.

MARGARET *pushes the baby buggy again up the slope.*

MARGARET. Freedom. The open spaces. The land at peace and high summer come. Hey ho my little loved one.

SHARON. My want an orange.

They go over the skyline. The Downs deserted. The kite flutters above.

A DOWN AND OUT MAN *comes on. He takes a bottle of Brown Ale from his coat. It is empty. He looks at it. His legs splay. He circles, rubbing the top of the bottle, he drinks as if rubbing the top had restored the contents. He looks at the bottle dismayed. He puts the bottle down on the grass. Above, the kite flutters. He looks up at the kite. He waves at it angrily.*

DOWN AND OUT MAN. Na. Na.

He pulls the lapels of his jacket up around his ears and, as if ducking from an assault from the air, he runs off. The Downs deserted. The kite above is still.

LORD RACK *comes on. He wears a fine but bulbous tweed coat, a homburg hat, ostentatiously large binoculars hanging around his neck beside their case. On his back there is an old army haversack. The neck of an unopened bottle of champagne pokes out of it. He carries another bottle of champagne which is nearly empty. He stands in the centre. His movements have parallels with those of the DOWN AND OUT MAN. He feels in his pocket for something. He looks up. He whistles huskily at the lark. He returns to fumbling in his pocket. He takes out a champagne glass. He pours himself a drink. He raises the glass in a toast.*

LORD RACK. Derby Day.

He drinks.

Eight a.m. Been up all night. Slept in the car. Picnic breakfast. Tummy churning already. It's a gut thing for me. The Common Man's race. They put me in 'House of Lords, but this is where I belong.

He takes a deep breath and coughs horribly. He sucks back phlegm and spittle. He scans the landscape through binoculars. He sees, in the distance, PRIMROSE, a traveller girl, come on. She carries a basket in which lie twigs of heather and pieces of silver-paper. She squats and puts the basket on the ground. She presses the pieces of silver-paper around the twigs of heather.

Ah. Life at one with Nature.

He strides and stumbles down the slope.

Good morning young lady. Don't take fright now. Just an old horse, out for a canter. Bit of a crib biter in my day, eh?

PRIMROSE *stares at him.*

Traveller are you? Or show people? Hard life. The concrete and the mud. I was on a House of Commons Select Committee for your folk. Aye. Did bugger all. Here, look here.

He fumbles in his clothing, takes out a wallet and takes from it a ten pound note.

Now don't shy and run off. Sell us a bit of lucky heather.

PRIMROSE *gives him a piece of heather. She reaches to take the note but he holds it back.*

Give us a bit of a cuddle. French kiss? Odds on you're not a girl who brushes her teeth, eh? Hey hey.

PRIMROSE *judges her moment then grabs the ten pound note, gives* LORD RACK *a rude sign — a suck of a finger, the finger held up — and runs off.*

Lust. It went in like a knife, many years ago, never to come out. Eh oh, get it over with, you silly old man. Get out 'press cuttings of your court case.

He takes out a wodge of delapidated newspaper cuttings. He rustles them.

Grubby wreathes and flowers — on the grave of a political career. Hey ho, read 'em. Promised your wife and 'Leader Of The Party in the House of Lords you would. Still. When you're caught with your trousers down and your cock in the till, that's all you've got left.

He turns the cuttings.

Oh the pain.

He turns the cuttings.

Down among the dirty vicars. On the page opposite the Leader in The Daily Telegraph. 'Labour Peer Found Naked In Curzon Street.' *(To himself.)* A trail of slime leads to back door of 'Bunny Club.

He looks up.

Mr Kite. When I was young, Mr Kite. I had ideals.

He sobs. He laughs. He controls himself.

I was kissed by Aneurin Bevan. In 1949. Great Welsh, slobby kiss. Ay. I was his brother in socialism. And I fought 'Ruling Class, I got my boot in in my day! I gave as good as I got! Ay well.

He stuffs the cuttings away and claps his hands.

That's the guilt back in the drawer for today.

He drains the bottle into the glass. He drinks. He takes a handkerchief from his sleeve and cleans the glass. He returns the glass to his coat pocket and the handkerchief to his sleeve. He looks about furtively. He places the champagne bottle next to the Brown Ale bottle.

The first breakfast done, of a glorious day.

He strides and stumbles off. The champagne bottle and the Brown Ale bottle on the Downs. The kite above flutters.

PEARCE comes on with JOCKS and HUGH, two stable lads. Both carry their shirts, stripped to their waists, and wear boxing gloves. JOCKS carries a bucket of water.

PEARCE. I won't pretend. I do have better things to do. But I will not have personal gripe between my stable lads. In the end it is the horses that suffer. And if the horses suffer, we all suffer. Is that staring you both up the arse as crystal fucking obvious?

HUGH. Yes Mr. Pearce.

PEARCE. Jocks?

JOCKS. What?

PEARCE. Is that staring oh never mind. Jocks, what is the matter with you? Family? Sick mother or something?

HUGH. He is a Red, Mr. Pearce.

PEARCE. He is a what?

HUGH. That is why he is so unpopular with the other lads, Mr. Pearce. Wants all the horses to go on strike, don't you Jocks.

PEARCE. Hughie, you really are a nasty little shit.

HUGH. Yes Mr. Pearce.

PEARCE. Are you a Red, Jocks?

JOCKS. What?

PEARCE. Dear God. Why does a sensitive creature like a horse get on with you so well.

HUGH. Sneaks out the cottage at night and licks their cocks. Don't you, Jocks.

PEARCE. All right!

HUGH. Can't have Reds in the Yard, Mr. Pearce!

PEARCE. Shut up! Right. Boxing match. My rules, every lad I employ knows 'em.

HUGH *leers.*

HUGH. Yes Mr. Pearce.

PEARCE. The two antagonists — in the open air — private place — bucket of water. Beat each other — one acknowledges defeat, pours bucket of water over himself — you come back, shake hands before me — then the three of us have a whiskey. I'll be on the 'phone in the Land Rover.

He backs away. He comes forward again close to JOCKS *and peers at him.*

I do hope you are as thick as you say you are, Jocks. I do hope so, very much indeed.

He backs away.

Well! Get on with it.

PEARCE *goes off, over the hill.* PRIMROSE, *with her basket and David Soul magazine, passes him. She sees* JOCKS *and* HUGH. *She sits down, a good distance away, and watches them. They do not notice her.*

HUGH. Hit me then. Go on.

Nothing from JOCKS.

I better hit you then.

JOCKS. If Pearce wants me bashed up, let him do it himself.

HUGH. What?

Nothing from JOCKS.

You give me the creeps. Ur, you're all sort of animally. The way you dribble. No, you're not even like an animal, you're like a fish. What you doing up here, on land with people? You ought to be in the sea, going glob glob with your fishy lips.

JOCKS. No point. Us hitting each other. And if we don't, who's to know?

HUGH. What a fishy thought.

JOCKS. Stupid.

HUGH. That's the way it is. That's the rules.

JOCKS. Stupid.

HUGH. And I've been really burning, you know? To have you swallowing your teeth in a pinky froth. It has been a real, burning ideal for me. A pleasure drooled over. Now one poke and I'm in heaven — and it's all a bit pissy.

JOCKS. Don't hit me then and I won't hit you.

HUGH. It's the rules.

JOCKS. Make our rules. Rules Pearce don't know about.

HUGH. You really are a little Red, in't you.

JOCKS. Don't know about that.

HUGH. Come naturally does it? Like B.O.?

JOCKS. Don't know about any of that.

HUGH. Oh brother, I've seen people go like you. And they go one way — straight out of racing. We don't fight — we get kicked out of Pearce's Yard — Pearce's Yard, one of the best — Pearce's mouth, very big — say you bad little indian, be lucky to muck out some old lady's nag at a Point-to-Point — savvy Kemo Sabay? So. What do you suggest?

JOCKS *picks up the bucket and empties the water over himself.*

Oh. Well. Fuck you. I mean, I know what you mean, but fuck you.

HUGH *gives him a 'V' sign and runs off.* JOCKS *looks up at the lark and whistles. He sighs. He sucks his teeth.*

JOCKS. It's hard. It's hard. And I like the horses.

PEARCE *appears over the skyline watching* JOCKS *through binoculars. He has a battered suitcase with him.*

PEARCE. Little fool. And he likes the horses, too.

PEARCE *strides down the slope to* JOCKS.

There is your card. There is your P.45. There are your belongings. There is one week's wages. Now get off.

JOCKS *stands there.*

Are you crying?

JOCKS. I'm wet all over aren't I.

JOCKS *kicks the bucket.*

PEARCE. That is highly unnecessary.

JOCKS *tears off the boxing gloves and throws them on the ground. He picks up his shirt and suitcase and walks away.* PEARCE *shouts after him.*

We are all on a billiard table Lad. Plink plink plonk. And we all end up — exactly where we are.

JOCKS. And who's putting the chalk on the end of the cue and going poke, eh?

JOCKS, *going over the skyline.*

PEARCE. You leave me cold Lad.

JOCKS *has gone.*

You can muck out sheep. All you're good for now.

He whistles at the lark.

Still there, birdy?

He picks up the bucket and the boxing gloves and goes off.

PRIMROSE *looks at her arms, then lies back covering her face with the David Soul magazine.* MINTY *comes on, dragging a car battery on the sack.*

MINTY. You'se old battery. Going to crack you like a nut. Get at that tasty lead in you.

PRIMROSE *snatches the magazine away.*

PRIMROSE. Oh Ma'am, what you doing?

MINTY. I bain't talking to you girl. You don't know how

dangerous that is, to go lying there shameless, all arms. When your Pa gets out the nick, won't he give you a wallop.

PRIMROSE. Oh Ma'am, let me lug that battery for you.

MINTY. Your Pa's tooken away, so I'll be the man. You sell that heather. And don't go getting green sludge off that grass on your new pants. And you go round with your sisters, when them crowds get up here. And I don't want you wearing that good apron. And I bain't talking to you.

PRIMROSE. Oh Ma'am —

MINTY. Nothing don't get me down. Not you, battery. Not a husband starry in Lowestoft nick. Not a girl acting the loobany in the grass. None of you get me down.

PRIMROSE. Don't go barmy Ma'am —

MINTY. We's the Gypsy Nation. You'se got to know that, gill. For you's own good. You don't know that, you'll end up some hedgecrawler nothing. So you get that silver-paper round that heather. We'se on these Downs to make a living and don't you forget it.

PRIMROSE. Barmy all day.

MINTY goes out of sight over the skyline.

Oh. Oh. Oh.

She calls after MINTY.

Ma'am! Don't you go breaking those batteries! Sell them to the dealer as they are! Just the men, showing off, when they break the batteries. To see the acid squirt on their boots. Ma'am? Oh. Oh. Oh.

My Ma'am always goes barmy. That's why she keeps on getting her teeth knocked out by men from the Council. When they come round and do things to us. Like pile earth up round the trailers with bulldozers, so Pa can't get the scrap out. Like get the Police to take Pa away. Break sewage pipes near-to so we all get the squits. Get boys off the estates to chuck stones. Set dogs on us. Burn us out. She goes barmy too when I say I want to marry David Soul. I've got all David's records. We've got hi-fi speakers in the trailer. But they don't work. But Pa said he'll meet a man at Epsom who'll sell him a transformer. But Pa's got tooken away. But he'll get out and it's not bad at Epsom. I may get married and all. But

not to David Soul, 'cos he's not one of us. Which is my hard
luck. And his.

She lies back with the magazine over her face. JOCKS *comes
on carrying his suitcase, his shirt held over his shoulder. He
looks at* PRIMROSE *from a distance.*

JOCKS. Little darling. Would I like to tear you to pieces. Ah ah,
don't touch the gypsy my old Grandma said. Eight uncles'll
jump out on your head.

MINTY *comes back on, over the skyline. She rushes down at*
PRIMROSE *and slaps her.*

PRIMROSE. Ow!

MINTY. I'll not tell you again. Get up off that grass, get that
heather done!

PRIMROSE. Ow Ma'am!

MINTY. I'll wallop you myself.

MINTY *slaps her again.*

PRIMROSE. Barmy old cow!

MINTY *slaps her again.*

MINTY. Don't you talk to your mother like that. And I'll have
that. Getting ways out of magazines.

MINTY *grabs the magazine.*

PRIMROSE. My pictures of David —

MINTY. That'll go on the fire. Pictures of men off the television.
You don't know where those ways'll lead you girl. You don't
know the dangers. The Gypsy got no friends in this world.
You just sell the heather and stay clear of men. And I don't
mean just in books. Now get to.

MINTY *strides up the hill.*

You'll not get me down, none of you. If I have to run from
one end to the other all day, you'll not get me down.
Batteries. Daughters.

She goes off over the skyline.

PRIMROSE. Barmy.

She rubs herself. She sees JOCKS. *She stiffens.*

What you gawping at?

JOCKS. Fancy a bit of heather don't I.

PRIMROSE. Oh yeah?

They stare at each other.

JOCKS. Come on the Fair with me?

PRIMROSE. You've got a hope.

JOCKS. See as far as Croydon off the top of the big wheel.

PRIMROSE. I said — you've got a hope.

JOCKS. Where's my heather anyway?

PRIMROSE *hesitates, then takes out a twig of heather from the basket and walks to him.*

PRIMROSE. Fifty p.

JOCKS. You're joking.

PRIMROSE. Take the Gypsy's luck or leave it.

She turns to go.

JOCKS. Here you are.

He fishes in his pay-packet and gives her a fifty pence piece. She gives him the heather.

Tell my fortune, I badly need to know my fortune.

PRIMROSE. Cross my palm with a five pound note —

JOCKS. Oh come on darling —

PRIMROSE. Pound then.

They stare at each other. JOCKS *takes out a pound note from his pocket. She closes his hand round the pound note.*

Have a wish.

JOCKS. You and me on the ghost train.

PRIMROSE. Don't tell me the wish. And don't make a stupid wish like that.

JOCKS *smirks.*

Wish then!

JOCKS *smirks again.* PRIMROSE *pulls at his hand, takes the pound note and opens his palm.*

You just got fired from your job.

JOCKS *takes her palm.*

JOCKS. You just got hit by your Mum —

PRIMROSE. You hate your boss —

JOCKS. You're none too pleased with your Mum, either —

PRIMROSE. You think you can go round do anything with anyone —

JOCKS. You want to go on the Fair.

PRIMROSE. You're going to end up with your teeth knocked out —

JOCKS. And you're going to end up going to the Fair.

PRIMROSE *pulls her hands away.*

·PRIMROSE. You don't know about us! You'se ignorant!

JOCKS. Gypsy, in't you. Steal washing off lines, don't you. Drink milk bottles on doorsteps and piss in the empties. Steal babies and eat 'em. Coming?

PRIMROSE. My Ma'am'll kill me.

JOCKS *shrugs and begins to walk away.*

(*To herself*) Oh. Oh. Oh. (*To* JOCKS.) Mister.

JOCKS *turns.*

We'll go separate to the Fair. Don't want my Ma'am seeing us from the camp, on the skyline. Find me by the big Wurlitzer.

PRIMROSE *goes off quickly, not looking at* JOCKS.

JOCKS. What d'you know? Lose my job. Pull a Gypsy girl. The ups and downs, the swings of life —

He goes off.

MR TILLOTSON *and* MISS MOTROM *come on. He is dressed rather shabbily in a sports jacket, open-necked shirt and flannels and scruffy brown shoes. She is dressed neatly in a cheap coat, black stockings and black shoes and wears a little hat. He carries a placard which reads 'NONE IN HELL.'*

MR TILLOTSON. If you do not like the text, Miss Motrom, you must say.

MISS MOTROM. I will, Mr. Tillotson.

MR TILLOTSON. In all honesty. As a fellow in Christ.

MISS MOTROM. I do not like the text.

MR TILLOTSON. But what's the matter with it? I was up all night, stopping the edges of the paint going furry.

MISS MOTROM. It is not that I do not like the text, Mr. Tillotson. It is more that it is not a text at all. It's more a saying.

MR TILLOTSON. It's the text of a saying.

MISS MOTROM. But not said by Jesus or Jehovah. Or the Apostles. Or anyone in the Bible. Actually, it was said by you.

MR TILLOTSON. 'None in Hell'. I think it's very much on the nail. Go down a bomb.

MISS MOTROM. Don't let's argue. It's a beautiful morning. Look at God's grass. God's air. And there's a lark.

They look up.

They could have builded a New Jerusalem here.

MR TILLOTSON. Yeah. 'Stead they builded a race track. I am not happy in my mind, Miss Motrom.

MISS MOTROM. But why not, Mr. Tillotson.

MR TILLOTSON. They bitching me, down the Mission? Putting the knife in, behind my back?

MISS MOTROM. They are good souls —

MR TILLOTSON. Prissy old dears. Who don't know sin from the back end of a bus. I know about Sin, Miss Motrom. I have seen it. I have done it.

MISS MOTROM. The congregation at the Mission are all with us, in Christ.

MR TILLOTSON. Yeah? Where are they then? Other Missions'll be here. Come lunchtime the punters won't be able to move for missions. Thick, the praises to the Lord will be.

MISS MOTROM. It was felt —

MR TILLOTSON. It was felt it was Jim Tillotson's idea. Come down here. Bear witness at The Derby. So it was given the holier-than-thou cold shoulder. And none of 'em turned up. Fucking about —

MISS MOTROM. Mr. Tillotson!

MR TILLOTSON. Sorry I'm terribly sorry.

MISS MOTROM. Mr. Till —

He lowers his placard.

MR TILLOTSON. See, I met my low here. At Epsom. For thousands it is a good day out, but for me — it is the grimy edge of the pit of hell, covered with ash. See, the root of my evil — the root of my evil —

MISS MOTROM. Jim, you don't have to talk about it.

MR TILLOTSON. I want to talk about it. *(He takes a long breath, lets it out.)* I was a gambler. I mean I really was a gambler. Some take it or leave it. But I had compulsion. Compulsive gambler, me. Have you any idea what that means? To get gambling money in my hands, I would have sold my children. I did sell my children. Where are they now? Twenty-four hour gambling! Ten-thirty, betting shop. The manager'ld keep my stool free. Bring me a cup of tea halfway through the afternoon, for I did not eat! Money was not for food! Never break a note, gambling money! Five-thirty, out the betting shop. Casino! 'Til four in the morning. Then — illegal casino! I have left a betting shop with twelve thousand pound in my hand! On to Soho, Windmill Street! Come the dawn, not a bus-fare. Oh, I was action man.

He takes a long breath, lets it out.

The end came at Epsom. Roberto's Derby. I motored down with this investment broker in his Rolls-Royce. Heavy gambling is a great leveller, a real brotherhood of ghosts. The second race gone, I'd done my money in. He nipped off for a pee. Know what I did? I sold his Rolls-Royce. To a bookie for ten thousand pounds. Come the last race I'd done that in too. Everyone was looking for me, wanting my blood. Investment brokers, bookies' runners. And I was marooned on the Downs all night. And caught pneumonia. And had my nervous breakdown. And came to Jesus. You don't know what I'm talking about, do you.

MISS MOTROM *(hard voiced).* My father had it.

MR TILLOTSON. Yeah but not the — real thing?

He looks at her.

MISS MOTROM. I was my father's mascot. He took me everywhere. I was seven the night he cleaned out six bookies at White City dogs. The runners were looking everywhere for us. We ran away from the stadium. My little blouse was full of five pound notes, the old white paper five pound notes? We got on a train to Brighton.

MR TILLOTSON. Casino.

MISS MOTROM. Casino. We booked into a lovely hotel. He had a heart attack in the bathroom. I stayed in the bathroom with him all night. He was dead. There were five pound notes all over the floor, like snow.

MR TILLOTSON. What did you do?

MISS MOTROM. Became an alcoholic. Until I was thirty. Then I came to Jesus.

MR TILLOTSON. Oh.

He nods.

MISS MOTROM. We're strong now. With Jesus.

MR TILLOTSON. Yeah. *(He raises the placard and looks at the text.)* Maybe 'None in Hell' is a bit — quirky.

MISS MOTROM. It will make a talking point.

MR TILLOTSON. Yeah that's the idea!

MISS MOTROM. Shall we go and have a cup of tea?

MR TILLOTSON. Yeah. And we'll leave some of the leaflets on the stall.

He takes her hand. She withdraws it at once, as if hurt. They walk away.

I don't know what we're going to do about hymns.

MISS MOTROM. We'll make do.

MR TILLOTSON. Bit difficult with two of us, to whip up a hymn.

MISS MOTROM. We'll make do.

They go off.

The Downs deserted. LORD RACK *comes on. He is eating half a chicken.*

RACK. The morning going wonderfully. Walked the course. Found a hamburger stall already serving. Had a couple and a hot dog. I'm up to breakfast number four and it's not yet half-past nine. Aaah. Always stuff myself on Derby Day. And if you sick up, why there's room for more. They don't understand that in Labour Party. Labour Party. Always thought of myself as a gentle, kindly man. Soft and sunny. But in politics they always called me a butcher. And I was! I have turned Division Lobbies into abattoirs. No no, I must not become sentimental, not upon the Holy Turf.

PEARCE appears at the top of the slope, carrying the boxing gloves and bucket of water.

Oh no. Not him.

PEARCE. Oh no. Not him.

RACK. Trainer Pearce, on the Downs.

PEARCE. Lord Rack, on the Downs. The red punter.

RACK. You crave the anonymity of a good day out — and that comes over the horizon.

PEARCE. Look the other way.

RACK. Look 'other way.

PEARCE. Scan the tree tops.

RACK. Let him see what a good time I'm having, and bleed.

PEARCE. A man who stands for everything I can't stand. Socialism and racing? Like an elephant trying to get up a nanny goat.

RACK. Managerial whizz kid. Selling his skills, not realizing how he is used. With his mod cons — horses stuffed with vitamin pills, poor animals badgered by swarms of accountants. Perverting 'sport of the common man.

PEARCE. Threatening my livelihood with 'tax the winnings' and lefty parrot cries. Without winnings how the hell are you going to improve the bloodstock?

RACK. Entertainment!

PEARCE. The bloodstock! I'm getting too angry. If I have to meet him now I'll make a fool of him.

RACK. He's going away.

PEARCE. No, what's the matter with you? We are on common land. Angels and worms, both have a right to the grass.

PEARCE begins to walk down towards LORD RACK.

RACK. No he's coming up. Bugger'll smell drink on me breath. I don't mind being a leper to the Racing Hierarchy, but why do they have to keep on coming up and ringing me bell?

LORD RACK *hides his half chicken behind his back. They stare at each other.*

PEARCE. Morning.

RACK. Morning.

They stare at each other. Then LORD RACK *takes a step back and* PEARCE *walks away.*

PEARCE. That went off all right.

RACK. That weren't too bad.

PEARCE. 'Spose the man is human.

RACK. You've got to be civil.

PEARCE. It's just a fact of life you live with — that the shits are always with us, like the poor.

RACK. Civil. While you store up your spit.

PEARCE goes off.

Hey hey. And now, I think — a visit to a bookie, a beer tent, bookie, another bookie, beer tent, beer tent bookie, bookie beer tent and bookie in that order.

LORD RACK *goes off. The Downs deserted.*

The kite flutters three times and falls to the ground. BOBBY *comes on and picks up the kite. He tests its tautness.* SANDY *appears at the top of the slope. He still smokes and carries a can of lager. He dribbles the football.*

SANDY. Football, Bobby.

BOBBY. I'm doing my kite, Dad.

SANDY. He is like a ghost in the midfield. And then from the deep it comes. The Trevor Brooking cross.

He passes the ball to BOBBY. BOBBY *ignores it.*

BOBBY. I'm doing my kite, Dad.

SANDY. Come on, the old one two. Set me up an overhead kick.

BOBBY. I'm doing my kite.

SANDY. Here. What's the matter with it.

BOBBY. It fell down.

SANDY. Let's have a look.

BOBBY *pulls the kite away protectively.*

BOBBY. It's a Kung-Fu kite, Dad.

SANDY. Four pound ninety-nine p. Bit of plastic and four sticks.

BOBBY. It's a Kung-Fu kite. In China they put bits of glass on the strings and cut down birds.

SANDY. Why?

BOBBY. 'Cos it's Kung-Fu.

SANDY *sighs.*

SANDY. Where's your mother?

BOBBY. Wheeling Sharon about.

SANDY. And where's your Grandpa?

BOBBY. Gone betting.

SANDY. At ten o'clock in the morning?

BOBBY. He said he knew a bookie.

SANDY. God almighty.

BOBBY. What's a gelding, Dad?

SANDY. What?

BOBBY. Grandpa says a gelding's a horse that's got its balls cut off.

SANDY. I must tell you about your Grandpa one day.

BOBBY. What's a prostitute?

SANDY. Well —

BOBBY. Grandpa says a prostitute is a woman who paints her nipples —

SANDY. Right! I am West Ham and you are the Arsenal.

BOBBY. Grandpa says you stuffed him in the Old People's Home. And you just get him out once a year to go to the Derby. 'Cos you and Mum have got a bad conscience.

SANDY. That's about it.

BOBBY. Why don't Grandpa live with us, Dad?

SANDY. Guess.

SANDY, *clapping his hands.*

BOBBY. Cos we haven't got anywhere to live! Cos we're living in the dormobile! In Mum's friend's garage!

SANDY. Ten out of ten.

BOBBY. How long we going to live in the dormobile, in Mike and Patricia's garage, Dad? Dad? Dad?

SANDY. Give it a rest, Bobby. We only been there eight weeks. While we look for something else. Do you mind living in the dormobile, Bobby?

BOBBY. It's great!

BOBBY *runs round in a circle, pretending the kite is an aeroplane.*

SANDY. You're great too. But why won't you play football with me?

SANDY *runs round dribbling the ball in a circle, the opposite direction to* BOBBY.

Oh control, oh grace —

BOBBY. Death in the sky —

SANDY. Utterly fit, utterly in tune —

BOBBY. Cut off their wings, down they fall —

SANDY. Harmony sings —

BOBBY. Death strikes —

MARAGARET *appears on the skyline pushing* SHARON *in the baby buggy.* SHARON *now clutches a green Kermit Frog.*

MARGARET. Your sainted father, Sharon. We have found him.

SHARON. My want an orange.

MARGARET. You cannot have an orange, lady-one-note. We'll play football with your Dad.

SHARON. NOT play football.

MARGARET and SANDY kick and pull each other over the football, laughing. They grab each other, fall and roll on the ground laughing.

BOBBY. She's got a Kermit Frog!

SHARON. MY WANT AN ORANGE.

MARGARET. Ask your father.

SHARON. My want an orange, Daddy.

SANDY. You cannot have an orange.

MARGARET. Because we have only got one left.

SANDY. Because we have only got one left.

SHARON cries. MARGARET and SANDY stop rolling and kiss.

Bobby — cheer your sister up.

At once BOBBY goes to SHARON and tickles her. SHARON tries to keep crying but cracks and begins to giggle. BOBBY pulls the Kermit Frog. SHARON resists. BOBBY stops. Then makes another pull. SHARON resists.

SANDY. Hang about, hang about. What's that thing?

MARGARET. A Kermit Frog.

BOBBY. I want a Kermit Frog.

MARGARET. It's for both of you Bobby. It's for both of you Sharon.

SANDY. How much did they knock us for that?

MARGARET. Three pound fifty.

SANDY. Bloody hell.

MARGARET. Derby Day?

SANDY. Oh yeah. Let's all go mad.

MARGARET. Let us do that.

They kiss and roll. Two buskers, BUD and MACK appear

on the skyline. MACK carries an accordion. BUD carries a paper bag.

BOBBY. I want to fly the frog on my kite.

SHARON. NOT fly my frog.

BOBBY. It's my frog too. They said. Be like an astronaut up on the moon.

SHARON. NOT fly my frog on the moon.

BOBBY *pulling the frog intermittently, SHARON resisting.*

MACK. Customers, Bud.

BUD. Right, Mack.

BUD *takes out a pair of dark glasses. Then a telescopic blind person's cane which he extends. Then a notice which he hangs round a little canvas bag on a wire hoop. Then a notice which he hangs round his neck. It is on a piece of black board, the letters are screwed-on garden gate letters. They read 'EX-JOCKEY ALMOST BLIND'. MACK strikes up 'When Irish eyes are smiling'. They advance confidently.*

They reach the family, who stare at them. MACK stops playing.

BUD. Ah — any musical requests?

SANDY. You've got to be joking.

BUD. Thank you thank you.

BOBBY. Play The Rolling Stones.

MACK. The Rolling Stones. Play The Rolling Stones.

BOBBY. Dad's always playing The Rolling Stones, in't you Dad.

SANDY. Shut up Bobby.

SANDY *puts ten pence in BUD's bag.*

BUD. Good luck. Follow The Minstrel today. Lester on The Minstrel. Look at the trainer's name. O'Brien! Follow the Irish today. Me old father were a tipster. I'll give you that one for free.

SANDY. Thank you very much.

BUD. Follow the Irish today.

The buskers shamble away, BUD on MACK's arm. BOBBY follows them, suspicious.

MARGARET. How much did you give them?

SANDY. Ten p.

MARGARET. Sentimental pig.

SANDY. Store up pennies in heaven.

MARGARET. The amateur gambler speaks.

SANDY. He does.

MARGARET. Three to one — that cloud will go over the sun.

SANDY. Mm — give you five to two.

MARGARET. Mm, five to two — subtle.

SANDY. Give you eight to one — there are ants crawling up — your left thigh.

MARGARET. Ah.

SANDY. Ah.

They kneel facing each other.

Maggy. Mike and Patricia wrote me a letter. It's getting bad, Maggy. I mean, they could come and talk to us. We are living in their garage.

MARGARET. Don't want to talk about it.

SANDY. And the dormobile's going to start smelling any day now. There's a limit to what half a dozen airwicks can do.

MARGARET. Not talk about it.

SANDY. They want to know when we're going to get a house.

MARGARET. We want to know when we're going to get a house.

SANDY. I don't blame 'em. They don't know about kids. And the scene in their bathroom does get pretty torrid. What with Bobby's theory about water going uphill. Jesus! If only I could get a set of aluminium ladders. I could set up and do roofing on my own. 'Stead of working off and on for any Dick and Harry. Ladders, light enough for one man.

MARGARET *looks up into the sky and closes her eyes.*

MARGARET. The airwicks. The bathroom. The ladders.

BOBBY. My Grandpa says buskers make a hundred pound a day. Are you really blind? My Grandpa says you live in big houses in Hampstead, surrounded by Alsatian dogs. My Grandpa says you keep your dirty clothes in the boot of a Rolls-Royce.

BUD. On your bike, sonny.

The BUSKERS *go off over the skyline.*

MARGARET. Buy ladders with the money in the Halifax.

SANDY. That four hundred pound's for a deposit Maggy. Hit that and.

MARGARET. And.

SANDY. Yeah, and.

MARGARET. Not be serious today. Frogs and kites and oranges today.

SANDY. Frogs and kites and oranges.

SHARON. MY want an orange.

SANDY. Have the orange my love! The last orange on earth! Why not?

MARGARET. Why not?

BOBBY. I want a Kermit Frog to fly from my kite.

MARGARET. Yes!

SANDY. Yes!

SHARON. My want a ginger biscuit with my orange!

MARGARET. Yes!

SANDY. Yes!

BOBBY. Dad, can I sit in the driver's seat in the dormobile?

SANDY. Yes!

BOBBY. With the, with the engine on?

SANDY. Yes!

BOBBY *dances in a circle, hop style, round* MARGARET, SANDY *and* SHARON.

MARGARET. We could — we could — put the money in the Halifax on The Minstrel.

MARGARET *and* SANDY *stare at each other.*

SANDY. You're a wonderful mother, Maggy.

MARGARET. It's eight to one — some gave nine —

SANDY. Ante post. It will shorten —

MARGARET. Four hundred pounds —

SANDY. A win, that would be —

MARGARET. Three thousand, six hundred pounds —

SANDY. Less tax —

MARGARET. Thirty-six times four p in the pound — hundred and forty so we would win — three thousand, four hundred and six pounds.

SANDY. If The Minstrel wins. It's mad.

MARGARET. Where have we got being sane?

SANDY. The deposit.

MARGARET. A garden.

SANDY. Aluminium ladders.

MARGARET. There'll be a Halifax in Epsom Town.

They stare at each other.

The trouble is — is The Minstrel going to win?

BOBBY. What you going to do, Dad? Dad, what you and Mum going to do?

MARGARET. Throw our lives away!

SANDY. Before the flashing hooves of a horse, going at forty miles an hour!

MARGARET. The right horse.

BOBBY. Great! Can I come?

GRANDPA WILLIAM *comes over the skyline talking. He wears a cloth cap and carries a tin lunch box and a small collapsible canvas stool.*

GRANDPA. Fifty-third Derby I have seen in my life. 'Cept in the last World War, when they ran it at Newmarket, on account of the Zeppelins. Or was that the First World War?

BOBBY. Grandpa! Grandpa!

SHARON. Grandpa! Grandpa!

SANDY. Oh dear. Here comes England's walking racial memory.

GRANDPA. The Derby's gone to the dogs. May as well be a dog race. I put it all down to that man on the telly, with the hat. He is in on the conspiracy to cheat the working man of his gambling rights.

BOBBY *dances around* GRANDPA WILLIAM.

BOBBY. We're going to throw ourselves in front of a horse and win a lot of money —

SHARON. Grandpa! Grandpa!

GRANDPA. They don't wear hats now, do they! You look in vain at the Derby crowd for a hat. Only the toffs wear the odd hat. And they do it to make the rest of us feel bad.

SANDY. Come on. Let's get down to our pitch. The two furlong marker.

MARGARET *and* SANDY *touch each other's hair.* SANDY *stands. He wheels* SHARON, *kicking the ball with* BOBBY *up the slope.*

BOBBY. Can I have an ice-cream?

SHARON. MY WANT ONE.

BOBBY. Can she have an ice-cream too?

SANDY. We will go down by the rail. By the magic strip of the grass. And you will eat ice-creams and your parents will consume many cans. It will be — like the beach!

SANDY *kicks the ball over the hill.* GRANDPA *follows them over the skyline.*

GRANDPA. In my day we all wore hats. If you saw a man walking down the street without a hat on, you'd all shout at him and say — oy! Look at him! He's got no hat on.

MARGARET *is momentarily left behind, picking up a child's clothing. The* GHOST *of Emily Davison comes on.* MARGARET *and the* GHOST *stare at each other.* MARGARET *goes off.*

GHOST. On the first day of June, nineteen-thirteen, Emily Wilding Davison got off the Derby Day train at Tattenham Corner Station. She held her coat around her. I held my coat tight around me. Beneath, around me, I had two flags, the green purple and white of the Movement. I had learnt the colours of the jockey who would ride the King's horse.

Purple and gold. Through the morning, through the crowd,
Emily Wilding Davison steeled herself.

The GHOST *goes off.*

*The Downs deserted. In the centre stand the bottle of Brown
Ale, the champagne bottle and* SANDY's *lager can.*

FOUR YOUNG MEN *and* TWO YOUNG WOMEN *appear on
the skyline. They are bedecked in Jubilee Regalia. They carry
carrier bags of beer bottles, drink from bottles. They hold the
edge of a large Union Jack. They run down the slope.*

ALL *(sing).* God Save our gracious LESTER
Long Live our noble LESTER
God Save our LESTER.
Happy and glorious long to reign over us
God save our gracious LESTER
God save our LESTER.

They go off.

SUPERINTENDENT BLUE *comes over the skyline, walking
across the Downs, talking into a walky-talky radio.*

BLUE. Everybody chop chop over.

The radio crackles a short burst.

If there is a tailback on the A24 because of some Gyppo
lorry stuck out of a B Road I do not want to know about it.
What the hell is he doing with a load of gas stoves on the
Downs on Derby Day anyway. Get him up on the verge, check
his breaks and book him. What about the A217 junction over.

The radio crackles.

If we do not move those vehicles we will have bookies going
down the white lines. What about that drunk who got off the
ten twenty-eight train with a heart attack, over.

The radio crackles.

He wants what?

The radio crackles.

·

No we cannot send a panda car for a roman catholic priest. What is our petty theft tally so far?

The radio crackles.

When will they learn. And there are three card tricks round the back of the toilets near the Rosebery Stand. Send a PC up to scatter 'em. And anyone seen the Chief Constable yet?

The radio crackles.

Well keep an eye peeled on the bushes.

BLUE *goes off.*

A BUNNY GIRL *comes on, with net tights and ears.* CHARLES PEARCE *comes on, nervous, looking at his watch.*

PEARCE. Come on come on.

The BUNNY GIRL *smiles at him.*

Did you say something?

BUNNY GIRL. Sir.

PEARCE *(to himself.)* Where are you, where are you? I'm a trainer of horses. Not a bloody butler.

PEARCE *looks at his watch.*

Your tail's on fire. There's a fish in your net stockings. Your ears are wilting.

BUNNY GIRL *(without changing her smile.)* I just stand here like this for the money. So don't give me a bad time you bastard.

PEARCE *stares at her.*

Here comes the helicopter now, Sir.

PEARCE. About time.

A MAN WITH BATONS — *like two orange table tennis bats — backs on to the stage. A whoosh of air and litter as a helicopter lands.* ROGER COYLE *and* DOROTHY DELAUNE *run on, crouching from the blades, their hats held to their fronts. They straighten, putting their hats on.*

DOROTHY. Charles.

PEARCE. Mrs Delaune.

DOROTHY. Do you know Roger Coyle? Charles Pearce my trainer, Roger.

PEARCE. How do you do.

ROGER. How do you do.

PEARCE. I knew your father.

ROGER. Did he know you?

DOROTHY. Roger!

BUNNY GIRL. Brochure, Sir?

ROGER. What?

BUNNY GIRL. Brochure, Sir.

ROGER. Your ears are wilting.

BUNNY GIRL. Thank you Sir.

DOROTHY. How is my darling, Mr. Pearce?

PEARCE. Frisky in his box, I am afraid.

ROGER (*to the* BUNNY GIRL.) There are fish in your net stockings.

DOROTHY. Roger! Forgive us, Charles. We are a bit merry.

ROGER. Quite. Breakfast was a trial.

BUNNY GIRL. Your car is waiting, Sir. Madam.

ROGER. Take it away. We will walk across the Downs. Bathe in the local colour.

PEARCE. I don't think —

DOROTHY. Roger, I've got you on a tight string. Don't forget it.

BUNNY. Your car is waiting.

PEARCE. It's getting a bit crushed down there in the dip —

DOROTHY. We will go by car.

ROGER. She is afraid she will get raped by the London poor.

DOROTHY. Don't play up Darling. No doubt the Daily Express is lurking in the bushes.

SUPERINTENDENT BLUE *comes on.*

BLUE Madam, your car is waiting.

DOROTHY. Thank you, Superintendent.

ROGER. All right! Roger Poodles will be a good poodle.

DOROTHY. I do hope we're going to have a good day, Charles.

PEARCE. Do you, er, want to look him over? Your horse?

ROGER. Later old man. Shampoo first.

DOROTHY *and* ROGER *go off.*

BLUE. Thighs worth two hundred thousand a year, stretching out of a helicopter onto the grass. Very arousing.

PEARCE. Huh.

BUNNY GIRL. Will her horse win?

PEARCE. A donkey versus the Concorde. Not that that woman cares. The owner of a Derby Runner. But to her just another handbag to chuck in the cupboard. (*To the* BUNNY GIRL). Look the other way, love.

The BUNNY GIRL *turns away.* PEARCE *takes out a hip flask.*

PEARCE. Alan?

BLUE. Not just now, Charles. One of the bigger moments of the day coming up. There is his chopper.

PEARCE. Who?

BLUE. The owner of Blushing Groom. The owner of the Derby favourite.

PEARCE. Not —

BLUE. The Aga Khan.

PEARCE. The Aga Khan. Oh my God.

The noise of the helicopter coming down is heard. THE BUNNY GIRL, PEARCE *and* BLUE *brace themselves, touching items of their clothing. The rush of air and litter rises and dies. The* AGA KHAN *comes on followed by his* DETECTIVE. *The* AGA KHAN *is dressed in black morning suit and hat and large, impenetrable dark glasses. The* DETECTIVE *wears dark glasses behind him, circling, a gun hand held to the button of his jacket.*

BLUE. Votre excellence. Je suis le Chef de Police du champ du course. Permettez-moi de vous accompagner à votre voiture.

AGA KHAN. Merci bien, monsieur le Chef de Police.

The AGA KHAN surveys the scene.

Pourquoi tout le monde agite-t-il le Union Jack?

BLUE. Ah. Ce sont les celebrations Silver Jubilee de notre Reine, votre excellence.

AGA KHAN. Un spectacle extraordinaire.

BLUE. C'est pour la gloire de la Patrie, votre excellence.

BLUE, *pleased with that.*

AGA KHAN. Tres jolie. Une image piquante de l'économie anglaise. Eh bien! Nous avons vu la scène, et maintenant — la victoire.

The AGA KHAN and his DETECTIVE walk away. BLUE follows.

BLUE. La voiture est là —

The BUNNY GIRL curtseys as the AGA KHAN passes. The AGA KHAN, his DETECTIVE and BLUE go off.

BUNNY GIRL. Every year they weigh him in diamonds.

PEARCE. Yes, he is a wonderful man. But for British Racing an Angel of Death.

BLUE comes back on.

BLUE. I'll have that nip now.

PEARCE *(handing BLUE the hip flask.)* He spends the money on the bloodstock. Why can't the Government learn that lesson?

BLUE *(to the BUNNY GIRL.)* Look the other way, love.

The BUNNY GIRL looks away. BLUE drinks.

PEARCE. Big winnings. The secret of success in racing.

BLUE. And in life.

BLUE burps and hands the flask back.

PEARCE. Forty-five million pounds of Government Subsidy a year to poofdahs poncing about in ballets and theatres. But

to a mass entertainment, beloved by all sections of the
Community? Ten million. No wonder foreigners win all our
races.

BLUE. Still. British horses are still born with four legs.

PEARCE. But for how long?

BLUE. Well! That's our bowing and scraping done. Drop you
both near a place of refreshment?

BUNNY GIRL. Ta.

They go off.

LES BACKSHAKER, *bookmaker, comes on with his wife*
CYNTHIA BACKSHAKER *and his settler* MORRY BURROWS.
*They carry their stand, boxes to stand on, big black bags with
chains and padlocks on them.* CYNTHIA BACKSHAKER *lays
out a blanket, on the blanket a fine table cloth, on the table
cloth an elaborate meal of cold lamb, chicken, salads, pâté,
cheese, with a champagne bottle in a silver bucket. She makes
sandwiches.* LES *and* MORRY *stand on their boxes.*
CYNTHIA BACKSHAKER *completes a sandwich and holds it
up to* LES BACKSHAKER. *He takes it, not looking at her. He
chews. This takes place during the* PUBLIC ADDRESS
SYSTEM's *announcements.*

PUBLIC ADDRESS SYSTEM. Here is an announcement about
crossing the course. Please do not cross the course.

The PUBLIC ADDRESS SYSTEM *plays 'The Sound Of
Music', played by a military band. The music stops.*

Do not drop bottles on the open Downs. Later on in the
day the Downs will be used by horses and children. After the
Meeting the Downs become an open space for the enjoyment
of the public. It is impossible to find glass.

The PUBLIC ADDRESS SYSTEM *plays 'The Sound Of
Music' for a brief burst.*

Please remember you can assist the organizers by not paying
more than twenty-five pence for an official race-card. There
are plenty of race-cards so please, insist.

THE PUBLIC ADDRESS SYSTEM *continues with 'The
Sound of Music'. The music stops.*

Do not place bets with bookies unless they are displaying
the official colours, the colours today are blue and white.

The PUBLIC ADDRESS SYSTEM *is silent.* MR TILLOTSON
comes on with his placard 'None in Hell'. MISS MOTROM
is with him. She carries a sheaf of leaflets. MR TILLOTSON
preaches, with halting and bizarre rhythms.

MR TILLOTSON. 'Gospel tracts everywhere.' Said a Youth.
With a sneer. As a young Christian Lad handed him a Gospel
tract. 'No not everywhere,' said the Christian Lad. 'There
will be None in Hell.'

MISS MOTROM. None in Hell.

MR TILLOTSON. God fastened that single sentence in the
Sneering Lad's brain. And ultimately he was converted.
There will be no tracts. No preaching. No second chance. No
Salvation. Not in Hell. I know. I've been there and looked.
And come all the way back. So. So.

The bookmakers have ignored them completely.

I think that went down very well.

MISS MOTROM. Very imaginative, Mr. Tillotson.

MR TILLOTSON. I'm not in the swing of it yet.

MISS MOTROM. More like this.

She is very aggressive and practised.
Meanwhile the bookmakers look one way, then the other,
chewing food impassively.

Lester Piggott? What horse does he ride? The Minstrel. Minstrel
means singer. But what song does he sing? Not the Lord's.
Not the Lord's song. Blushing Groom is the favourite today.
But what does he blush for? Right — sin. Not for happiness.
Hot Grove is the third horse fancied here today. But is that
a grove of trees in the garden of Gethsemane? No, it is a hot
grove of flames in Hell. There is only one race being run here
today, brothers and sisters. The Race Of Life. And only one
winning post. The cross of Jesus Christ.

MR TILLOTSON. Very good.

MISS MOTROM. Shall we go and have a hot dog?

MR TILLOTSON. I will buy it for you.

MR TILLOTSON *and* MISS MOTROM *go off.* LES
BACKSHAKER *belches loudly.* MORRY BURROWS *belches
loudly. A* VENDOR *comes on selling paper cups with a string
hanging from the bottom and a polyester, crudely cut chicken
stuck on top. Rosin applied to the fingers resonates the cup
in a loud, chicken-like noise. He makes the noise.*

VENDOR. Jubilee chicken! Get your Jubilee chicken! Get your
Jubilee chicken here! Buy it and cherish it for years! Your
Jubilee chicken!

The VENDOR *goes off.* LOUIS, *another bookmaker, comes on,
carrying a bookmaker's bag.*

LES. Oh no. That's my day ruined.

MORRY. Bottle it up, Les.

LES. That bastard.

MORRY. Just carry it off. Bottled up.

LES. I will bottle it up. It may come out of my ears, but I will
bottle it up.

MORRY. And we'll get him later in the day.

All smile.

LES. Hello Louis!

LOUIS. Hello Lesley!

LES. You know Morry Burrows. The Morry Burrows.

LOUIS. Hello Morry, how's the lung?

MORRY. The fucking bastard's knife, third and fourth rib —

LES. Now now, bottle Morry. He's very good about his wound.
He's practising yoga. Mental control. Sucks the cigar smoke
in one lung and not the other. How's the family, Louis?

LOUIS. You know how it is, Lesley. The worm in the bud.

LES. Making money?

LOUIS. A drizzle of pennies.

They laugh. Frost. LES *and* LOUIS *take out cigar cases.*

Cigar, Lesley?

LES. Have one of mine Louis!

LOUIS. No you go ahead.

LES. No you go ahead.

LOUIS. I insist.

LES. That is very tough, Louis. So do I.

LOUIS. Smoke our own.

LES. All right.

LOUIS. No. Have we not known each other long enough?

They simultaneously take a cigar from each other's case and light up.

LES. So. You have left the big boys in Tattersalls. Come down here amongst we small fry.

LOUIS. My son-in-law is holding the fort in Tattersalls. I thought a day on the Downs would do me good, with the little punters. Don't want to lose the common touch.

LES. It's God's grass —

LOUIS. God's air —

LES. God's money —

They laugh. They pat each other. They suddenly grip each other's arm. LES nearly topples from his box.

LOUIS. We got to end the feud between our families, Les.

LES. Oh really?

LOUIS. The tide comes in on us all.

LES. Does it?

LOUIS. I know I've done a bit better than you, over the years. And I don't mind a niggle. But not all this blood.

LES. What blood?

MORRY. Blood from the tyres on his Rolls-Royce he means.

LOUIS. That was you at Sandown, then. Lesley Lesley. This is the era of the Horserace Betting Levy Board. V.A.T. All the Romeo and Juliet stuff — rumbles on Brighton beach, that is obsolete.

PUBLIC ADDRESS SYSTEM. Please, if you must cross the course, please use the tunnel opposite the Rosebery Stand or the official crossing at Tattenham Corner. The police will help you. Thank you.

LOUIS. Can you even remember why we hate each other? Eh?

> LES *and* MORRY *look one way then the other.*

> Good luck to you then. Brother. Morry. (*To* MRS BACKSHAKER.) Cynthia.

> MRS BACKSHAKER *does not look up, continuing to prepare food.* LOUIS *goes off.*

MORRY. Incredible.

LES. God Almighty.

MORRY. The pip.

LES. Almighty God.

> LES *and* MORRY *look one way then the other.*

MORRY. Why do you hate his guts?

LES. I can't remember.

> LES *and* MORRY *burst into laughter.* LORD RACK *comes on. He looks through his binoculars at the bookmakers.*

LORD RACK. Two big bookmaker crows on the gate. Hey hey, lunch underway. Time to make a bet on The Derby.

> LORD RACK *pats his clothing.*

> Lucky rabbit — little Indian God — bit of Newmarket turf tucked in me knickers — right — just get at one with 'universe.

> LORD RACK *kisses his hand and touches the earth, then paces about with strange, erratic steps.*

> Before betting on a classic race — I always try for two days — never to step on a crack in 'pavement — and when I approach 'bookmakers — to never stand on a patch of bare earth — and never to speak to a woman wearing red —

LES (*to* MORRY). Oh my God, look at that. (*Aloud.*) Watch it Lads! Here comes a betting man! It'll be the workhouse for us all! (*To* MORRY.) Telephone the bank manager — get him to clear out a few cupboards.

> LES *and* MORRY *giggle.*

LES. Good morning my Lord.

RACK. Gentlemen — I come to lay myself upon that bed of nails — the on course odds.

LES. What does he take us for, Morry?

MORRY. Bookmakers, Lesley.

LES. How do these slanders get about?

RACK. I have observed a close correlation between the pulpit and the bookies stand —

LES, RACK and MORRY. Men kneel before both.

RACK. What do you fancy for The Derby then, Lesley?

LES. Ah. Now. There's a curly one.

RACK. Never will say will you, bookies. The only true professional gambler is a bookmaker. And he never loses.

LES. I run a public service. We are the dream-weavers are we not, Morry?

MORRY. Like fuck.

LES. Quite right. We're just here to make a bundle. A bet on The Derby, My Lord?

RACK. Forty quid on Blushing Groom.

LORD RACK *gives* LES *four ten pound notes.*

LES (*to* MORRY.) Ticket number sixty seven. Forty pound to one hundred pound, The Groom.

RACK. What will you give for Milliondollarman?

LES. Milliondollarman, sixty-six to one.

RACK. I'll go twenty quid, each way.

LORD RACK *gives* LES *four pound notes.*

LES (*to* MORRY.) Same ticket. Twenty pounds to one thousand, three hundred and twenty pounds to win, and for a place — one fifth of the odds —

MORRY (*with no hesitation.*) Two hundred and sixty-four pounds.

RACK. That's all.

LORD RACK *steps away. He thinks again and returns with a zig-zag manoeuvre.*

Look, er — I'll have thirty quid each way on Lucky Sovereign. You know, flags everywhere. And Liz motoring up 'course later on. Be a shame not to.

LES. Patriotic. And the horse may win. Lucky Sovereign, twelve
to one. (*To* MORRY.) Ticket number sixty-eight. Thirty
pounds to three hundred and sixty pounds to win, and for
a place —

MORRY (*with no hesitation.*) Sixty-two pounds.

RACK. That's me, gentlemen.

LES. My Lord.

LORD RACK *strides away with his superstitious step.*

Amusing little bet.

MORRY. Hundred and eighty quid. Better lay it off, Les.

LES. Let's see. Blushing Groom? It's not going to stay. No
matter what they say. First three, maybe. But he bet to win.
Milliondollarman? Be the marker, won't it. Front runner down
the hill, busting its bollocks to exhaust The Groom. Lucky
Sovereign? Three legged guinea pig. Still, we'll lay it off.

MORRY. On the safe side.

LES. What other side is there?

MORRY. Bloody socialist. He should get back to Russia. What's
he doing, sitting in the House of Lords anyway? Bloody insult
to the Queen.

LES. What a man of parts and passions you are, Morry.

MORRY. Don't know why you take his bet.

LES. A bet is a bet.

MORRY. Oh yeah, you must have your pound of flesh. You
don't need a bank account, you need a deep freeze.

LES. Thank you, Morry. Thank you. I needed that.

MORRY. There is a code.

LES. There is no code.

MORRY. There is a code.

LES. There is no code. There is only the punters — twenty-
five p. or a hundred and eighty quid. And there is the strength
of locks upon my bag. And there is the threat of powerful
friends with knuckles.

MORRY. All right, all right!

LES. It gets to me! Talk of codes. We all want the same thing, right? Us. The mugs. The boss in the Club Stand, glass of champers in his hand. The working man on the Downs, in his hand a doctor's sick-note. And what do we want? Why, just a big front room. Cocktail cabinet in the shape of the World. Malt whiskey and pearly telephones. And all the rest — codes — is a bit of a mashed turd.

LES *eats*.

Five to two the field. Five to two the field.

GRANDPA *comes on. He sets his little stool by the two-furlong marker and sits upon it.*

GRANDPA. Queen Victoria. Silly old bugger. Silly old cow. Thought the world owed her a living. I tell you what was really weird about Queen Victoria. She couldn't bear to look at a gardener. Buckingham Palace gardens of a morning, when she came out after breakfast, for a smoke, all the gardeners had to duck down behind the rhododendron bushes. She could not bear to see a gardener working. If she saw a gardener working, she fired him.

MARGARET *wheels SHARON on in her baby buggy with BOBBY. MARGARET carries a rug and plastic bags containing food. She begins to lay out the rug and food.*

BOBBY. We going to have the picnic now?

MARGARET. When the Queen's gone by.

BOBBY. She gone by now?

MARGARET. No Bobby, she has not gone by now.

A POLICEMAN takes up his position standing on the course.

GRANDPA. 'Nother funny thing about Queen Victoria, she had the Royal chinese laundry wash her black widow's weeds two times a day.

MARGARET *stares at* GRANDPA.

MARGARET. What?

SHARON. Mummy? What is the grass?

MARGARET *stares at* SHARON.

MARGARET. What?

SHARON. What is the grass, Mummy?

A young man, a JUBILEE DRUNK, *bedecked in Union Jacks and wearing a Union Jack cardboard top hat comes on. He carries bottles of Guinness.*

MARGARET. Make your frog jump up and down, Sharon. See, he's all flobbily.

SHARON. Flobbily.

JUBILEE DRUNK (*to* MARGARET). Alone with all your brood, darling?

MARGARET. Go away.

JUBILEE DRUNK. Don't give me a hard time.

LES. You heard the lady. Waddle away.

JUBILEE DRUNK (*backing away*.) No offence. It's just me. That's all.

He goes a distance away and stands drinking.

LES. It was a plague of ladybirds last year. This year it's Jubilee Drunks.

MARGARET (*to* LES). What are you giving for The Minstrel?

LES *taps his board.*

LES. Lester seven to one darling.

MARGARET. Will that price get any shorter?

LES. That depends upon the market. Before market forces, we are but trees in the wind.

MARGARET. But very much shorter?

LES. You want to read minds, Gypsy Lee is in her caravan.

GRANDPA. Funny thing about coppers. They hate you calling 'em copper. (*To the* POLICEMAN.) Hello copper!

POLICEMAN (*relaxed and smiling*). Grandad. Lovely day for it.

LES. Thinking of a little bet on The Minstrel then darling?

MARGARET. My husband's gone into town. To get it out. Of the Building Society.

LES. Big time. You know where to come.

MARGARET. I do.

LES *eats*.

GRANDPA. You got flat feet, copper! Your whistle's bunged up, copper!

MARGARET. Grandpa!

GRANDPA. You got tramlines on your Y-fronts!

MARGARET. Grandpa!

POLICEMAN. You have a good day, Grandad. All of us have a good day.

BOBBY. He doesn't hate it, Grandpa. He likes it.

GRANDPA. That's because they've all been threatened by Scotland Yard. I saw 'em, over the other side of the coaches, in a little wood. All sitting on the grass, in ranks, having a cup of tea. Being threatened — like it or else.

MARGARET. Sorry. He's an old aged P.

POLICEMAN. Don't worry love. He earned it, let him enjoy it.

BOBBY. When's the Queen coming?

POLICEMAN. She'll be along.

BOBBY. Copper!

MARGARET *slaps* BOBBY's *leg*. BOBBY *yelps*.

MARGARET. And don't step on the rug, Bobby. Kneel on it.

BOBBY *glowers and flops to his knees*.

GRANDPA. It is a lie I've got it in for the Queen. It's just her forebears I've got it in for. Because their hands are stained with English blood.

BOBBY *is fishing in a bag*.

MARGARET. Bobby don't poke in the food!

MARGARET *hits* BOBBY *again. He yelps*.

JUBILEE DRUNK. Showing a nice bit of leg there darling!

BOBBY. I want to go on the Fair!

SHARON. Mummy, what is green? Mummy, what is green? What is green, Mummy?

MARGARET. Green is green!

BOBBY. You and Dad never let me go on the Fair!

SHARON. Why is green green!

GRANDPA. I'll say this for the Queen. At least they nationalised this one.

MARGARET, *a knife covered with butter, looks up to the sky.*

You can tell that by the arm she waves with. And here I am letting all and sundry into a bit of privileged information. That arm is a mechanical arm, operated by the Central Electricity Generating Board, a nationalised industry. Therefore that arm is an advance for Socialism, of a kind.

LES. Five to two the field.

GRANDPA. Though I still say chop it off.

JUBILEE DRUNK. No offence darling?

He toasts MARGARET *with a Guinness bottle.*

BOBBY. I'm kneeling on the rug Mum. I'm not poking in the food Mum. So can I go on the Fair?

SHARON *throws the Kermit Frog onto the course.*

LES. Oy! Behave yourself!

JUBILEE DRUNK. Oy oy!

MARGARET *ignores the incident. The* POLICEMAN *picks up the Kermit Frog.*

POLICEMAN. Now now Kermit. What's a frog doing in The Derby?

The POLICEMAN *throws the frog back.*

Don't let the kids throw things over the rail, love. Bit of sense.

JUBILEE DRUNK. Here comes Liz to see The Derby.

MORRY *stands, he and* LES BACKSHAKER *raising binoculars. The* POLICEMAN *comes to attention.* BOBBY *strains to see.*

BOBBY. That's not the Queen that's a car.

GRANDPA. They put her in a car.

LES. A Daimler.

MORRY. She is wearing blue with white accessories.

JUBILEE DRUNK. The Loyal Toast.

A tableau of these figures as the Queen's car approaches down the course — unseen in the play. MARGARET *still kneels on the rug, the buttery knife in her hand. The* MRS BACKSHAKER *actress has become the* GHOST *of Emily Davison.*

GHOST. It's only a white rail. You could jump. Push the copper over. Crack the windscreen with your knife.

MARGARET. It's got butter on. Be blood and Anchor butter, all over the place.

GHOST. England at peace on Derby day. It is just a picture, thin as paint. Slash it.

MARGARET. What's the point? They're bound to have a spare Queen in the boot.

GHOST. See the dirty wall behind.

MARGARET. I don't mind making the food. Bobby likes coleslaw sandwiches. Coleslaw is twenty-seven p. a tub, in Sainsbury's.

GHOST. I saw the wall. In a flash. A second before the king's horse smashed my skull. Did I do that for you to sit on the grass and make sandwiches?

MARGARET. There is nothing wrong with being a mother, there is nothing wrong with making the food, there is nothing wrong with sitting on the grass.

GHOST. No. Everything is wrong.

In silence — the figures in the tableau raising their arms and opening their mouths to cheer. A blackout.

Act Two

The parade ring. A HORSE *is being led around by a* STABLE LAD.

HORSE. I am a Derby outside chance.

They parade.

The mentality of a race horse can be compared to the mentality of a bird. Nervous, quick, shy and rather stupid.

The HORSE *flashes his teeth at the spectators. The* STABLE LAD *restrains him.*

STABLE LAD. Don't give me a bad time.

HORSE. Many a racehorse has a fixed idea. Chewing blankets. Kicking buckets over. Biting blacksmiths.

They parade.

My fixed idea is that I must have a goat tied up with me, in my box. And there, tied to a stick in the Yard, when I come back from the gallops. I will kick the place down, if I don't have my goat.

They parade.

Where is my goat?

They parade.

I want my goat!

STABLE LAD. Stop thinking about your bloody goat!

Owners walk gracefully into the parade ring — a SVELTE
VOICED MAN, *a* HARSH VOICED MAN, *a* SMOOTH
VOICED WOMAN *and a* SWEET VOICED WOMAN. *The
men are dressed in grey morning suits and top hats, the
women in fine clothes and fashion hats.*

SWEET WOMAN. It is so difficult, when you go small, to find
any rooms to lock things up.

SMOOTH WOMAN. But we must meet before Ascot. If only for
tea and cakes?

SWEET WOMAN. Not before Ascot. Perhaps in September? My
diary is a traffic jam.

SMOOTH WOMAN. One's life does flow over. (*She looks at the*
HORSE.) When I look at a race horse, I always think of
footballers' legs. So lean and tight.

SWEET WOMAN. Mm.

HORSE. Goat?

SVELTE MAN. Nervous?

HARSH MAN. Can't stop going to the bog.

SVELTE MAN. What owning a race horse in The Derby is all
about.

HARSH MAN. Bowels like ice-cream and hot chocolate sauce.

SVELTE MAN. Owner's tummy. Get sloshed.

HARSH MAN. I am sloshed. It never shows in my family.

He gives a little stamp of his foot.

God! I want to win this race. On this fat, lazy afternoon.

SVELTE MAN. I'm just here for the fat, lazy tax loss.

HARSH MAN. I do love the sport too, you know.

SVELTE MAN. Oh we all love the sport.

SWEET WOMAN. Here comes our jockey. Doesn't he look a
little pea on a drum?

The owners turn toward a JOCKEY, *who comes on dressed
in silks, crash helmet and cap, riding boots and carrying
a whip. The* JOCKEY *actor walks upon his knees.*

JOCKEY. I walk out into the ring. A professional. Weighed on the scales. Ready. Sharp. All there. I have eaten one piece of toast since dawn. It lies now beneath my diaphragm. Which is taut and hard as leather. I feel the eyes of Lords and Ladies upon me. The owners and trainers. The Chairman of Boards. The yellow eyes of the mug punters, the piss-pots and the know-alls, the down-and-out and the cracked. And I clench my arse for action.

The owners turn away. The JOCKEY *walks to them. He touches his cap.*

SVELTE MAN (*to the* JOCKEY.) Spruce and raring to go?

JOCKEY. It'll be a good long ride.

The HARSH VOICED MAN, *the* SVELTE VOICED MAN *and the* SWEET VOICED WOMAN *stand around the* JOCKEY. *The* SMOOTH VOICED WOMAN *looks away.*

SMOOTH WOMAN. One does feel contempt for the people who look at one, around the parade rings. From the quay-side at San Tropez. It is hard not to. People are such silly empty dustbins, gaping. And I could fly above them, if I wished. On that slicky feeling of a perfect day.

PUBLIC ADDRESS SYSTEM. Will the Jockeys please mount for the third race, the Epsom Derby Stakes. Will the Jockeys please mount.

The STABLE LAD *leads the* HORSE *to the group of owners. The* SMOOTH VOICED WOMAN *runs her hand down the* HORSE's *body.*

SMOOTH WOMAN. So elegant and within himself.

The two men help the JOCKEY *to mount the* HORSE.

SVELTE MAN. Just let him go naturally down the hill, old man.

JOCKEY. Sir.

HARSH MAN. That's right. Let his nature come out to the fore.

SWEET WOMAN (*sharply*). Stay away from a horse with blinkers. And if you are within shouting distance come the last two furlongs, let us not be over-confident because he naturally drifts to the right. The tilt of the ground may yet fool him. And you.

JOCKEY. Ma'am. (*Aside.*) You wade through the bullshit — then, at last, you get where you belong.

The HORSE *and his* JOCKEY *are led away by the* STABLE
LAD *to circle the parade ring again. The owners watch the*
HORSE, *turning in a group.* PRIMROSE *and* JOCKS *come*
on. She carries a Kermit Frog in one hand and a stick of
candyfloss in the other.

JOCKS. There you are. The parade ring at The Derby. Three
kinds of animal, and all bred for it. The horses, bred for it.
The little men to ride the horses, bred for it. The owners
of the horses, bred for it.

PRIMROSE. Don't look like they're having much of a good
time.

JOCKS. They're having a good time all right. They just button
it in.

He looks sideways at her.

Hold my hand then.

PRIMROSE. Not round here.

JOCKS. Trip on the big wheel? Kermit Frog, candyfloss, visit
to the parade ring? Ought to be a hold of a hand in that.

PRIMROSE. I said, not round here.

JOCKS. Show the bastards we don't care. And it's public, if you
pay your money.

PRIMROSE. A Romany girl does not hold hands. It's not decent.

JOCKS. All right, all right. Don't go up the wall.

They watch the parade ring scene for a while.

PRIMROSE. You can have a lick of my candyfloss.

JOCKS. Oh very sexy.

He tries to bite the candyfloss.

PRIMROSE. Not while I'm holding it!

JOCKS. Oh dear oh dear.

PRIMROSE *gives the candyfloss to* JOCKS *who takes a bite*
out of it.

The JOCKEY *rides the* HORSE *out of the parade ring.*

JOCKEY. Hup!

HORSE. Oh good! I'm going to see my goat!

The owners drift off slowly.

SVELTE MAN. Did you see that ridiculous little man, in the Club Stand, take his hat off late when the band played The Queen?

HARSH MAN. Yes. Did you hear what that other ridiculous little man said to him?

SVELTE MAN. No. What?

HARSH MAN. He said — you are a ridiculous little man, take your hat off. They both left, ashen in the face.

SVELTE MAN. Ridiculous.

The owners go off. JOCKS *and* PRIMROSE *alone.*

JOCKS. I'll never get back in. I look at them, the way they walk over the grass — and know I'll never get back in. Horses get on with me. It was the human beings kicked me in the face. Marry me.

PRIMROSE *takes a step back.*

PRIMROSE You watch your lip.

JOCKS. Why?

PRIMROSE. You gone wrong in the head?

JOCKS. Not that bad an idea. I know horses. You're all off to Appleby Horse Fair next week. I'll come and live with you. Be a Gypsy.

PRIMROSE. We're travellers. We call us that, not you.

JOCKS. I'll talk to your father.

PRIMROSE. Pa's away —

JOCKS. Talk to your mother —

PRIMROSE. My Ma'am'll set the dogs on you. I will and all.

JOCKS. All right, I'm joking.

PRIMROSE. You don't know our life!

JOCKS. All right!

PRIMROSE. Gorgios, you're filthy!

JOCKS. All right I'm not joking! They chuck you and your trailers on dumps, right? And where am I? Six foot high would-be jockey, ex-stable lad — with the bad mouth on him? Chucked on a dump.

They stare at each other.

Both of us, shoved out the door aren't we?

They stare at each other.

If you won't marry me, least come out over the Downs. Show the bastards we don't care. Give us a lovely long fuck in the grass, eh?

PRIMROSE *throws the Kermit Frog at* JOCKS *with all her strength. He catches it, startled.*

PRIMROSE. You don't know anything of us. How we get by. What we do. My Ma'am were right. You're filthy.

JOCKS. Just hold hands —

PRIMROSE. You don't know what we do. You're filthy.

PRIMROSE *runs off.* JOCKS *looks at the candyfloss and the Kermit Frog. He circles, embarrassed.*

JOCKS. Asked for that. Me who has worked in stables? Try to pull a Gypsy girl on Derby Day? For that bigger men than I — have had their hearts and their kneecaps broken. Oh well.

He tosses the Kermit Frog and the candyfloss away. He takes out his paypacket.

Two pound, eighteen p. left. And I went and bought her a frog. I have got to get a grip on my affairs. Two pound, eighteen p. Maybe you'll stay dead still up there, sun. And The Derby'll go on forever. And I'll live on the grass. And a kind old — hamburger fairy godmother'll come and feed me And lovely Gypsy girls'll wash me all over. *(He looks at the money.)* I think I'll put a pound on Lester. And blow the rest in the beer tent. Then, just before the last race — the Revolution will break out. And there will be a mass distribution of the profits of William Hill Limited.

He clenches the money in his fist.

Oh God. What am I going to do?

He calms himself.

Lester. Beer tent.

Outside a beer tent. LORD RACK. *He clutches bottles of light ale. Bottles of light ale are at his feet. A woman with a* LOUD VOICE *is ordering drinks, waving a ten pound note high in the air. Two* DRUNKEN YOUNG MEN *writhe around each other, unable to stand as they try to pull a crate of beer away.*

RACK. The great race looms. A bright banner unfurled, among half a million punters.

LOUD VOICE. Who wanted a brandy? There was someone who wanted a brandy. What? There was no one who wanted a brandy.

1ST DRUNK. Just get this — down to the Lads on the rail.

2ND DRUNK. What we got to do — is get this down to the Lads on the rail.

1ST DRUNK. I've got an idea. Let's get this down to the Lads on the rail.

RACK. This is what I want. I suck back every moment.

JOCKS *approaches.*

I know you. Stable Lad. In Pearce's Yard.

JOCKS. Oh yeah.

RACK. Have a drink with me.

JOCKS. I'm all right.

RACK. Nay. Ten minutes to the great race. First wave of boozing at its height — ride the crest, Lad, while you can. What are you having?

JOCKS. Light ale.

LOUD VOICE. No. Four gin and tonics, not five. Don't bother to open the lagers. And a Coca-Cola for a kiddy.

1ST DRUNK. We've got a problem.

2ND DRUNK. There is no problem.

RACK. The betting and the boozing. Deep seated social habits. There is something magnificent in deep seated social habits. I do not accept there is anything evil.

The 1ST DRUNKEN YOUNG MAN *peers at* LORD RACK.

1ST DRUNK. Here. That's Robert Morley.

2ND DRUNK. That's not Robert Morley.

1ST DRUNK. It's Robert Morley.

2ND DRUNK. That's not Robert Morley. Robert Morley's a teetotaller.

1ST DRUNK. Never. Is he?

RACK. Why, George Wigg himself said to me — George Wigg with his sleeves rolled up, yanking the balls off the Jockey Club — he said to me, what did he say to me?

JOCKS. I —

RACK. I do not accept there is any evil. That is what George Wigg said to me. And he was right! The punter's got a lot to thank George Wigg for. First man to take on the Jockey Club. Tell the Duke of Norfolk what he could do with Norfolk. George Wigg wrenched the Horserace Betting Levy Board out of grip of 'English Aristocracy. Bought Epsom Downs for 'Nation. Helped the Common Man have a bet on street corner with dignity. Good on you George. We love you Lad.

LORD RACK *lurches*.

LOUD VOICE. Oh for godsake. People are drinking in here.

RACK. Take British Leyland. You know what the lavatories are in British Leyland? Betting shops. I don't tell a lie. The lavatory attendant in there, he's a runner for William Hill's! They should open a betting shop, middle of the shop floor. Bingo, all problems solved. Lives brightened.

JOCKS. What about the Stable Lads' strike, in nineteen seventy-five?

RACK. Don't heckle me Lad! Were you with that lot?

JOCKS. I was at the back of the crowd. When George Wigg came down to Epsom, to talk them out of it.

RACK. Shouting?

JOCKS. Having a drink.

RACK. Ah yes, but — he were right. Don't think I don't feel with you lad. You can't disrupt Derby. National Asset. The damage to the image of Britain abroad — too horrible to contemplate. Exports. What you don't realise is, a British victory in The Derby, that's worth more internationally — than gunboats up the Nile ever were. You've got to have vision. And another thing. Derby belongs to everyone. See, ordinary men and women are cut off from decision making. Only time in their lives they make a decision — is having a bet on a race like The Derby, in local betting shop.

JOCKS puts the bottle of beer down, walks away and goes off. LORD RACK does not see he has gone.

If I had my way in betting shop. They'ld have carpets. Colour tellys. Nice lights. Little — bar at one end. Coffee, sandwiches, ale. Play-pen for the kiddiwinks.

The woman with a LOUD VOICE walks away, laden with drinks. The two DRUNKEN YOUNG MEN are making progress across the grass.

LOUD VOICE. They are always there. Every year. Labour life peers. Chewing through the canvas of the Tattenham Corner beer tent. I point them out to Japanese tourists, as part of the local colour.

The woman with a LOUD VOICE goes off.

RACK. Brighten their lives. All I wanted. I do not accept there is any evil.

1ST DRUNK. Get down to the Lads.

2ND DRUNK. Right. But we'll just get down there to the Lads.

PUBLIC ADDRESS SYSTEM. And now the runners for the one hundred and ninety-eighth Epsom Derby Stakes, the Jubilee Derby, are parading before the Grandstand — in the order in which — they appear on your race-card.

LORD RACK has slid to his knees.

RACK. Oh you gambling nation on the grass. Come to graze at Epsom Races. Dreaming things will look up. That gates of Paradise will open — on 'flash of an horse's hoof. I love you all — and I'm sorry I let you down.

1ST DRUNK. I'm going to bloom my cheeks.

2ND DRUNK. You're what?

1ST DRUNK. I'm going to flash my arse.

2ND DRUNK. Yeah, but we got to get down —

1ST DRUNK. I want to. It's The Derby.

2ND DRUNK. Yeah?

1ST DRUNK. Here we go!

2ND DRUNK. Oh dear oh dear.

The 1ST DRUNKEN YOUNG MAN *drops his trousers and flashes his behind in* LORD RACK's *direction. He waves an arm in recognition.*

1ST DRUNK. Eh up!

2ND DRUNK. Eh up!

RACK. Eh up and good luck!

The TWO DRUNKEN YOUNG MEN *and* LORD RACK *go off, leaving beer bottles behind.*

The JOCKEY *comes on, riding the* HORSE.

JOCKEY. You ride out, over the Downs. To the mile and a half start. Of the Epsom Derby Stakes.

HORSE. Where are you, goat?

JOCKEY. Don't you, you bastard.

HORSE. Goat.

The JOCKEY *smoothes his hand upon the* HORSE.

JOCKEY. And suddenly it is peace. Twenty-two professionals, twenty-two animals. In the countryside. For the first time for hours, you hear the birds. And over the hill there waits for you — a tunnel of your own fellow human beings. Out of their minds with joy.

The JOCKEY *rides the* HORSE *off over the skyline.*

The GHOST *of Emily Davison comes on.*

GHOST. Emily Davison pushed through the crowd at Tattenham Corner. Stood by the rail. She watched her thoughts — I watched my thoughts, like lights over a marsh, flaring on the grass. King George the Fifth's horse, Amner, was halfway down the field when they reached Tattenham Corner. Emily ducked under the rail onto the course. Stood with her coat open. Opened her arms. The horse hit me. My skull was cracked. The jockey broke a rib. I lay in a coma for five hours before I died. The Queen sent a telegram asking after Emily. The King refused to do so. He sent a telegram asking after the jockey. Stupid Emily. Rash Emily.

The GHOST *goes off.*

Two TICK TACK MEN *and two* BOOKMAKERS *appear above. The* 1ST TICK TACK MAN *whistles.*

2ND TICK TACK MAN. You what?

The 1ST TICK TACK MAN *whistles and signals again.*

You what? Oh got you.

The 2ND TICK TACK MAN *whistles to the* 1ST BOOKMAKER.

Alf! Alf!

1ST BOOKMAKER. Nine to four the field!

2ND BOOKMAKER. Nine to four the field!

1ST BOOKMAKER. Nine to four The Groom!

2ND BOOKMAKER. Lester, five to one!

1ST BOOKMAKER. Get your money on Lester, girls. Five to one The Minstrel!

Below MARGARET *pushes* SHARON *in her baby buggy. They are in a lavatory queue.* SHARON *holds her Kermit Frog.*

MARGARET (*to herself*). Come on queue.

SHARON *stares.*

SHARON. Mummy, why — the men waving money?

MARGARET (*to herself*). Ooh God.

SHARON *stares.*

SHARON. Mummy, why — the man and the lady doing lying down?

SHARON *stares.*

MARGARET (*to herself*). A simple, common garden piss.

SHARON. Mummy, why — man on the bus throwing beer? Mummy —

SHARON *stares about for something to stare at.*

Why that policeman running? Why that fat man laughing?

Why that man and that little girl doing dancing? Mum!
Do dancing with me!

MARGARET. Not now.

SHARON. Why?

MARGARET. Do dancing with your frog.

SHARON. Dance stupid frog.

SHARON, *making the frog dance manically.*

Dance dance dance.

MR TILLOTSON *comes on with his placard, 'None In Hell'.*

MR TILLOTSON. Miss Motrom. Got split up in the crowd. Miss
Motrom. Got lost. (*To* MARGARET.) 'Scuse me Mrs. You
seen a religious lady going in that toilet?

MARGARET *looks at him, then looks away.* MR TILLOTSON
stumbles a distance away.

I want a bet. The marrow in my bones wants a bet. The
action all around me. I can't breathe.

SHARON. What's that man want, Mum?

MARGARET. He just believes in God, Sharon.

MR TILLOTSON. I can go through the whole field.

He takes a deep breath.

Fourty to one, Baudelaire. Sixteen to one, Be My Guest.
Eleven to four, Blushing Groom, favourite. Twenty to one,
Caporello. Twenty-eight to one, Gairloch. Ten to one, Hot
Grove. One hundred to one, In Haste. Twenty-eight to one,
Lordelaw. Eight to one, Lucky Sovereign. Thirty-three to
one, Milliondollarman. Thirty-three to one, Milverton.
Thirty-three to one, Monseigneur. Hundred to one, Mr Music
Man. Ten to one, Nebiollo. Fifty to one, Night Before. One
hundred to one, Noble Venture. Sixty-six to one, Pampapaul.
Twelve to one, Royal Plume. One hundred to one, St.
Petersburg. Hundred and fifty to one, Sultan's Ruby. Five
to one, The Minstrel. Eleven to one, Valinsky.

He rests on his placard stick, panting.

1ST BOOKMAKER. Eleven to four the field!

2ND BOOKMAKER. Eleven to four the field!

1ST BOOKMAKER. Get your money on The Derby!

2ND BOOKMAKER. Five to one Lester!

1ST BOOKMAKER. Comes but once a year!

2ND BOOKMAKER. Eleven to four the field!

MR TILLOTSON *rummages in his pockets.*

MR TILLOTSON. I'll just do The Minstrel. Fifty p. each way.
And an outsider. Or two outsiders. And Blushing Groom on
the nose. Oh —

He stops still.

I'm breathing again.

He rushes off.

2ND BOOKMAKER. Come on girls, get your money on Lester!
Five to one!

1ST BOOKMAKER. Lester, the housewife's fancy!

2ND BOOKMAKER. Let Lester be your tipple, ladies!

The 1ST TICK TACK MAN *whistles.*

1ST BOOKMAKER. What? What?

1ST TICK TACK MAN. Alf! Alf!

1ST BOOKMAKER (*to himself*). What's he trying to say? Oh,
Hot Grove's gone eleven to one. (*He shouts.*) Hot Grove,
eleven to one! Willie Carson's horse, eleven to one! Willie
Carson, another ladies' man!

SANDY *comes on.*

PUBLIC ADDRESS SYSTEM. Please keep pets, dogs, children
and other animals under strict control. Thank you.

SANDY. I got the money out. Three hundred and ninety-nine
pound. I left a pound in. Terrified I was going to miss the
race. The Manager had to telephone London. Then the
traffic back from the Town — like a squeeze box. Maggy?
I got the money in my socks. Squelch squelch on our future.

He sits down, pulling at his socks.

PUBLIC ADDRESS SYSTEM. And now the riders are arriving
behind the stalls.

SANDY. They'll be off. I've got to get our bet on.

MARGARET. Your bet.

SANDY. Maggy, what's the matter?

MARGARET. I've got a headache.

SANDY. Get down to our pitch on the rail, Maggy. Grandpa will be swamped down there. They go woomph, up to the rail when The Derby starts.

MARGARET. I'm queuing to go to the loo.

SANDY. Maggy —

MARGARET. I'm queuing to go to the Ladies' Lavatory.

SANDY. Don't bitch me! Not when we've had a good day.

He takes two handfuls of bank notes out of his socks.

I'll go and get the bet on. Yes? No? Tell me.

SHARON *looks from her mother to her father to her mother and bursts into tears.*

Get down to the rail, Maggy. I'll make the bet. Yeah? Go and piss in the grass. I feel like a worm.

SANDY *goes off.* SHARON *continues to cry as* MARGARET *speaks.*

MARGARET. I love The Derby. I always have loved The Derby. But in this queue, with my child yelling, waiting for a common garden pee, I hate The Derby.

She looks up to the sky and closes her eyes.

I hate the fat, happy people on the grass, with their teeth stuck in chicken drums. Jubilee flags coming out of their hairy ears. Minds red with booze and bets. I hate the little men in pretty colours, who go by on the horses, with their mean, hard little heads and mean, hard little bums. I hate the penguins in the grandstand we gawk at through binoculars. I hate the race officials whizzing along the other side of the rail in their yellow car, chinless wonder masks behind the glass. I hate the jolly boys on the tops of the buses, roaring pissed, stripped to their navels, showing off their lovely tummies in the sun. I hate the coach party lovers. The totties that are pulled. The marriages that are made beneath the great wheel at the fair. Oooooh I begin to hate my fellow men and women, squeezing my insides, keeping my knees together in this queue. Trying to think of something else. If I get a pee, will I join in? Have a good time again? Love my husband and my children again? Love the crowd by the rails again? Not feel choked by the gas, rising over the crowd, the gas of a good time had by all — oooooh, come on Sharon. Let's go and have a piss in the grass.

MARGARET *runs off pushing* SHARON *who, still crying, waves her frog round her head.* MR TILLOTSON *comes on.*

PUBLIC ADDRESS SYSTEM. And the runners are going into the stalls — now.

1ST BOOKMAKER. The Derby comes but once a year!

2ND BOOKMAKER. One minute before they go!

1ST BOOKMAKER. Lester, still five to one!

MR TILLOTSON. Seven bets on. So sweet. Like warm blood. And easy. Like Our Lord, walking on water.

2ND BOOKMAKER. Blushing Groom, gone out to three to one now! Three to one the favourite!

MR TILLOTSON *hunts in his pockets.*

1ST BOOKMAKER. Ten to one, Hot Grove!

2ND BOOKMAKER. Ten to one, Lucky Sovereign!

MR TILLOTSON. Lucky Sovereign? Jubilee year? It can't fail. I got to get it on.

MR TILLOTSON *runs off.* MARGARET *wheels a happy* SHARON *on.* SANDY *comes on from the other side.*

PUBLIC ADDRESS SYSTEM. All the runners are in the stalls now.

MARGARET. The Derby, Sandy.

SANDY. The Derby, Margaret.

SANDY *and* MARGARET *embrace, he lifts her and swings her in an arc.*

SHARON. My want — see The Derby.

SANDY. Come on then!

They run off, MARGARET *pushing* SHARON. *The stage is deserted.*

PUBLIC ADDRESS SYSTEM. The flag is up. They are under starter's orders — now.

The stage deserted. THE DERBY *played by one actor, comes on over the hill. The actor is festooned with the regalia of the race.*

THE DERBY. I am the Epsom Derby Stakes.

Being —

Twelve tons of twenty-two horses and twenty-two small men —

Boots, bridles, crash helmets, weights and whips — silks and light underwear —

Each horse carrying nine stone —

The lot worth twelve million pounds sterling plus —

A race for three year old horses, run over one and a half miles —

Begun over a hill, behind trees, where no one can see a blind thing that's going on.

THE DERBY *strides over the hill out of sight. The* DERBY COURSE *comes on. He smokes a cigarette in a long holder, wears a summer suit with two-toned shoes and carries a cut turf in the palm of a hand.*

THE COURSE. I am the Derby Course. Don't be fooled by lush green curves in the countryside. I am dangerous. I am a bad-tempered bastard. I bite legs. On me the second-rate burst blood vessels and heart valves. Only the fast, the brave and the beautiful get anything out of me. First, I am a killer gallop, up a long hill. Then I sweep down, curving to the left, to the real ball-tearer, a vicious left-hand corner, Tattenham Corner, turned at forty miles an hour. Then the straight run to the finish, but down another hill. And at the last hundred yards — the ground falls away from the Stand into the farside rails. That's me. Switchback. Twisty. Feared by the hardened man and animal. To win the Derby — out-think me. Then kick my brains in. Or I'll break you apart.

The actor lays the turf in the centre of the stage. A CROWD, *rushing to the rails, comes on. Among the crowd is*

MR TILLOTSON. *He carries his 'None In Hell' placard. The* DERBY COURSE *actor joins the crowd.*

FIRST CROWD

MAN IN THE CROWD. Get down on the rails now, don't take no for an answer, woomph!

THE DERBY *out of sight.*

2ND MAN. Where are they?

3RD MAN. Miles away, over behind us.

4TH MAN. Henri Samani, my dreams go with you!

MR TILLOTSON. I've got it. That trembling feeling. They're going to go, any moment now.

1ST WOMAN. I can't see anything. Just grass.

2ND WOMAN. You'll just see 'em when they go by.

3RD WOMAN. Where's Lester? Annie, where's Lester?

2ND WOMAN. He's not gone by yet! You'll know him, when he does. He's got an arse like a little cream bun.

4TH MAN. Henri Samani! My life is in your hands.

3RD MAN. How much you put on him then?

4TH MAN. Fifty p.

MR TILLOTSON. My tongue's gone furry! I'm going to be sick, I'm going to die, no I'm not! Oh Jesus Christ Our Lord forgive me I've bet on The Derby and I'm in Heaven!

PUBLIC ADDRESS SYSTEM. And they are off.

THE DERBY *actor begins his display of the race.*

THE DERBY. Clang go the gates!

Leap goes twelve tons of horse and men!

AND it's Baudelaire the first to show. Frankie Durr that tough little walnut on top. Then Lucky Sovereign, the no-hope offspring of the great Nijinsky, the Jubilee mug punters' tipple. Then Milliondollarman, then Nebiollo, the Two Thousand Guinea winner — is this horse a paper tiger?

AND now it's Milliondollarman on the farside, neck and neck with Baudelaire and Lucky Sovereign going up to join them.

Just in behind comes Nebiollo, then Caporello, then Be My Guest.

Who's going to blow it going up the hill? Who's going to take up the running? What the fuck is Lester Piggott doing?

The CROWD *runs to another position, as if six furlongs from the start at the top of Tattenham Hill.* MR TILLOTSON *keeps his position. The* CROWD *leaves litter behind.*

MR TILLOTSON. The action is what a gambler craves for. Two and a half minutes the race lasts, but I'll hold my breath and the action will go on forever.

MR TILLOTSON *takes a deep breath and his cheeks puff out.*

SECOND CROWD.

1ST WOMAN. Why we got to stand on the hill?

2ND MAN. Always watched The Derby from here. You see 'em come up and you see 'em go down.

1ST WOMAN. Why can't we watch the finish?

2ND MAN. Cos you got to pay ten quid and dress up like a bloody penguin.

2ND WOMAN. I'm pregnant. I'm pregnant.

3RD WOMAN. Don't tell me, tell your husband.

2ND WOMAN. Ted — I'm pregnant.

3RD MAN. What?

2ND WOMAN. I wanted to tell you. When The Derby goes by.

3RD MAN. Great. If it's a boy we'll call it Lester.

2ND WOMAN. What if it's a girl?

3RD MAN. We'll call it Lesterine.

THE DERBY *coming into sight.*

THE DERBY. And suddenly all the jockeys know. Baudelaire is buggering himself up the hill, giving them all the ride.

AND as they race up to the top of the hill it's still Baudelaire — Gairloch makes a challenge but falls back, broken by the speed. And breaking the hearts of his owners, Mr Paul de Moussac and Miss V. Hermann-Hodge.

Baudelaire continues the ball-breaking gallop on the inside, Royal Plume comes to challenge but being driven hard by Joe Mercer.

AND it's Royal Plume from Valinsky, Milliondollarman, Caporello.

AND to the outside — Blushing Groom, the Aga Khan's horse. Never beaten in its life. The favourite. The wonder horse.

And looking to the back markers it's Sultan's Ruby. Lordelaw. And in among the stragglers — Lester Piggott on The Minstrel.

3RD MAN. Where the hell is Lester?

4TH MAN. At the back. Like a monkey on your spine, waiting to pounce.

THE DERBY. And Night Before pulls up. Pat Eddery pulls up Night Before. A blood vessel burst.

THE DERBY *screams.* THE DERBY *actor arranges the* CROWD *into positions of the field.*

They race over the top of the hill. Baudelaire disputing it with Milliondollarman. Valinsky makes ground on the inside. Right up with them — Caporello and Lucky Sovereign and Noble Venture. Just in behind them, Willie Carson on Hot Grove. Behind Hot Grove, Henri Samani on Blushing Groom, well placed on the inside. Behind Blushing Groom, Lester Piggott on The Minstrel.

(*Aside.*) Lester — sneaking up from the back, to sniff the bollocks of the French favourite.

1ST JOCKEY. What the fuck is Lester doing?

2ND JOCKEY. Go down the hill you bugger.

3RD JOCKEY. What's that cunt trying to do to me?

4TH JOCKEY. Keep cool you beauty, you fucker.

5TH JOCKEY. For fucksake, someone bust that frog horse now.

6TH JOCKEY. Mille fois merdes.

7TH JOCKEY. Shit.

The CROWD *runs to another position as if on the inside of Tattenham Corner.* MR TILLOTSON *lets out a big breath and pants. The* CROWD *leaves litter behind.*

MR TILLOTSON. It's got to me again, every bit of my body. Gambling, I'm sorry I walked out on you.

THE DERBY. Milliondollarman from Baudelaire. Caporello. Lucky Sovereign.

In behind them — Be My Guest, Valinsky, Nebiollo, then Blushing Groom. Losing ground — Royal Plume. The backmarker is — Mr. Music Man.

AND at the front Milliondollarman takes over the lead!

THIRD CROWD.

1ST MAN. Milliondollarman! Sixty-six to one! I'm going to be rich!

1ST WOMAN. I want my kid to see The Derby!

2ND WOMAN. Hold her up then.

A CHILD, *played by the* 3RD WOMAN, *burst into tears within the* CROWD.

2ND MAN. Come on little girl. See The Derby. Tell your dollies all about it when you get back home.

THE DERBY. Hot Grove makes progress on the outside, Willie Carson like a pea on a drum.

AND they round Tattenham Corner. Where a jockey can utterly lose his bottle and the race. ~~And a horse on the inside rail can have his hide peeled like a ripe tomato.~~ Milliondollarman. Hot Grove. Caporello third. Baudelaire fourth. And fifth, the Minstrel coming strongly.

(Aside.) ~~Lester's brain ticks — like an intercontinental ballistic missile, on trajectory.~~

The THIRD CROWD *produces Union Jack flags in a tableau — the* CHILD *is held up above crying. At the back of the* CROWD *a* STREAKER *bares his behind.*

THE DERBY. Milliondollarman from Hot Grove, to face the hill down to the finish.

The crucifixion of the horse that won't stay begins.

The CROWD *runs to another position shedding litter to form the* FOURTH CROWD *around* MR TILLOTSON.

GRANDPA *sits at the front of the* CROWD, *on his little canvas stool, impassive and silent.*

Three furlongs to run in The Derby. Milliondollarman is pressed by Hot Grove. The Minstrel in third place. Then Be My Guest.

AND Blushing Groom unleashes a run. Henri Samani asks the question.

(Aside.) Will the French favourite stay? Bred by Red God out of Runaway Bride. But Red God never did more than a mile. Genes in the animal's chromosomes grind and shudder.

Two furlongs to run in The Derby.

FOURTH CROWD.

THE DERBY. It is Hot Grove from The Minstrel. Then Blushing Groom still making progress. Monseigneur moves into fourth place. Hot Grove from The Minstrel from Blushing Groom.

The FOURTH CROWD *shouts the names of* HENRI, LESTER, WILLIE, THE MINSTREL, HOT GROVE *and* BLUSHING GROOM, *as* THE DERBY *passes them.* GRANDPA *on his stool, silent.*

THE DERBY *is past the* FOURTH CROWD, *which strains to see the finish.*

The closing stages of the nineteen seventy-seven Epsom Derby Stakes.

Blushing Groom has nothing left.

Willie Carson on Hot Grove thinks the race is his.

Then Lester Piggott — lets the reins slip two inches through the palms of his hands.

The Minstrel responds. A bat out of hell, bullet out of a gun, the lash of a whip.

A hundred yards to run in The Derby. Lester Piggott and Willie Carson. The Minstrel on the near side, Hot Grove on the far side.

AND in the last second, like throwing a knife through a doorway as the door slams — The Minstrel wins.

THE DERBY *walks off.*

PUBLIC ADDRESS SYSTEM. Photofinish. There will be a photograph.

MR TILLOTSON. The Minstrel's Derby. I'd tear my eyes out to bet on a race like that again.

MR TILLOTSON *studies his race-card feverishly. The crowd disperses, stunned, to become the* FIFTH CROWD, MARGARET, SANDY *and* GRANDPA *amongst them.*

FIFTH CROWD.

MARGARET. Sandy. We won.

SANDY. Maggy. Aluminium ladders.

1ST WOMAN. First I saw the race — just like a crowd of bees.

2ND WOMAN. What happened?

2ND MAN. They call for a photograph when it's under a length. But the word is definitely Lester.

The 3RD MAN *starts and runs off.*

SANDY. Take a picture of me.

MARGARET. We've not got a camera.

SANDY, *holding the winning ticket to his chest.*

SANDY. Someone take a picture of me. I won The Derby.

MARGARET. Someone take a picture of my husband.

SANDY. For crying out loud what am I doing? Let's get to that bookie.

SANDY *takes* MARGARET's *hand. They run off.*

1ST WOMAN. Like bees, on the horizon. Then they were dead in front of me. All whips and froth. Then just grass again.

A couple embrace.

PUBLIC ADDRESS SYSTEM. Here is the result of the third race, The Epsom Derby Stakes. First number twenty-three, The Minstrel. Second number six, Hot Grove. Third number three, Blushing Groom.

The couple lie on the grass, embracing.

MR TILLOTSON. The four twenty. Lester's on Golden Libra.

MR TILLOTSON *goes off*

GRANDPA. Lester Piggott? Win The Derby on The Minstrel?
What good's that to the working man? Five to one, less tax?
No good at all. Bloody conspiracy. That Lester Piggott. That
trainer from Tipperary. Got together with that man on the
telly with the hat. Done the working man in, yet again. The
Minstrel? Drifts to the left. Oh well. Derby done. Heavy
boozing starts.

GRANDPA *packs up his stool and goes off. Necking couples
on the grass. A cascade of litter falls from the roof of the
theatre to the grass.*

MR TILLOTSON *and* MISS MOTROM *appear. She hits him
over the shoulders with the 'NONE IN HELL' placard.*

MISS MOTROM. Fallen.

MR TILLOTSON. I just had a little bet, Miss Motrom.

She hits him again, knocking him to the ground.

MISS MOTROM. Man fallen. Man turned against the light. Man
in his own filth.

She hits him repeatedly on the behind.

MR TILLOTSON. But I backed The Minstrel.

MISS MOTROM. And on how many other horses did you
squander God's given pennies?

MR TILLOTSON. The whole field. Ow.

MISS MOTROM. And what about the rent? And the collection
at the Mission? And a cup of tea even?

MR TILLOTSON. All right, I did my money in.

MISS MOTROM. Did The Lord in.

MR TILLOTSON. Ow.

She is exhausted. She sags. She sits back down on the grass.

I sold the return half of my train ticket. To a wino for ten p.
I had to make up a fifty p stake. To put on Milliondollarman.
A horse with a name like that, could it fail?

MISS MOTROM. Could it?

MR TILLOTSON. Came eighth.

MISS MOTROM *searches amongst the beer bottles.*

What are you going?

MISS MOTROM. I want a drink.

MR TILLOTSON. No look, don't do that —

She scours the bottles on the stage, holding them up against the light to see if there is any drink in them.

Don't Jenny.

MISS MOTROM. I want a drink.

MR TILLOTSON. You'll end up hating yourself, and all that.

MISS MOTROM. I do hate myself, and all that.

MR TILLOTSON. We'll both go down then.

MISS MOTROM. We went down long ago.

MR TILLOTSON. Let's have a prayer.

MISS MOTROM. I want to have a prayer. No, stuff prayer.

She sucks at empty bottles.

MR TILLOTSON. Ooh. Eh, Jenny. You've given me religion, right at the base of me spine. Don't do that. For pity's sake.

He knocks a bottle out of her hand. She slaps him, he slaps her. They clutch each other's hand.

MISS MOTROM. What are we going to do, Jimmy?

MR TILLOTSON. Pub? On to an all night casino? Then dice with the winos on Waterloo Station, 'til the betting shops open, eleven o'clock in the morning?

MISS MOTROM. I want to kneel down and pray —

MR TILLOTSON. That's no good, religion? A hypodermic needle called God. I mean I tried to get it in me — the manger and the tomb. I've just ended up punctured all over, running sores of goodness up my arm —

MISS MOTROM. You've got to flood your life with Jesus. If you don't, you'll just flood it with beer.

MR TILLOTSON. We could just try — and get back home. And have a cup of tea. If you'ld, er, lend me the train-fare.

MISS MOTROM. Never lend to a gambler. Just give.

MR TILLOTSON. Tattenham Corner Station. Don't know if I'll make it. There'll be crap games spilling out from the Fair all over there.

MISS MOTROM. There are three public houses between here and Tattenham Corner.

They look at each other, holding hands loosely.

MR TILLOTSON. Give it a whirl, then.

MISS MOTROM. Go it alone.

MR TILLOTSON. Hack through the jungle.

They go off.

JOCKS *alone on the Downs, picking through the litter.*

JOCKS. Huh. Huh. Huh.

PRIMROSE *comes over the skyline.*

PRIMROSE. What you doing? Stable boy. Mister. Gorgio lover.

JOCKS *continues to pick through the litter.*

You gone daft or something?

JOCKS *straightens.*

JOCKS. I'm looking for a Tote ticket. Someone who got a winner. Or a double. Or a jackpot, who knows? Maybe they dropped their ticket. And I can find it. And have their winnings. For my train-fare. Off this place. Right?

He bends.

PRIMROSE. Got no money then.

He straightens quickly.

JOCKS. I was going to back The Minstrel. But I had a rush of the blood to the head and backed Royal Plume. Royal Plume came in last.

He bends.

PRIMROSE. Do you want a job?

He straightens slowly.

JOCKS. You what?

PRIMROSE. For ten pound.

JOCKS *stares.*

JOCKS. What job?

PRIMROSE. Not saying. You take the money. Then you do the job.

JOCKS. Work for some Gyppo? What do you want me to do? Shovel shit?

She looks at him.

No no, I. Bit low. Just working up to walk to London. They did it, the last century. Thousands out of the East End on foot. To see the race and back again. Christ are we soft!

He kicks at the litter.

PRIMROSE. Say yes. Get the money. Do the job.

She takes a ten pound note from her sleeve. He looks at the note, shrugs and takes it

JOCKS. What's the job?

PRIMROSE. Job's in two parts. First part — kiss me.

They kiss. They step back from one another.

JOCKS. Ah — what's the second part?

PRIMROSE. Go away.

She turns and goes off quickly, over the skyline.

JOCKS. Right.

JOCKS goes off.

LORD RACK crawls over the skyline.

RACK. Fell asleep! On the Downs! Oh. Have I been robbed?

He rolls on one side, then the other, patting his pockets.

Car keys. Notebook for me autobiography. Day's winnings — seventeen pence. Ey. To go through card on every race, and still end up even? That's maturity of judgement. Right.

He struggles to his feet.

Go and sleep it off in 'car. Perfect end to a perfect day. Hey, after a day's racing like that, even an old atheist, socialist life peer has to say — God's in his heaven and all's right with the world.

He falls over, back down the slope out of sight.

SUPERINTENDENT BLUE *and* CHARLES PEARCE *walk on over the skyline.*

BLUE. Evening stroll. Wind down. A civilised idea, Charles.

PEARCE. I do it every year, after The Derby. To lick my wounds.

BLUE. Poignant.

PEARCE. What?

BLUE. The litter.

PEARCE. Common ground. And look what they do to it.

BLUE. Be back to nature tomorrow morning, for another day's racing. The inmates of the local asylum will see to that.

PEARCE. Always found it in bad taste. Turning the loonies loose to clear up.

BLUE. A Derby Day tradition. They look forward to it. Bit of a bear with a sore head, aren't you Charles?

PEARCE. I made a foolish remark earlier in the day.

BLUE. What? Oh yes. If The Minstrel wins The Derby, you will eat the Pope.

PEARCE. Marry. Marry the Pope. I was going to eat the Pope if Blushing Groom won The Derby. Well, I've been tipped off. Somehow that remark has got into tomorrow's Daily Express.

BLUE. Don't let it get you down. I'm sure his Holiness is a very nice girl.

BLUE *shuffles a toe through the litter.*

PEARCE. I am a man at the top of my profession. Before I crawl to the Pearly Gates, dragging my ulcer behind me, I will win the Blue Ribbon of Racing. Even an MBE. Why, then, am I not calm? Why do I feel — abused?

BLUE. Relax, take up Sunday painting. I have. Scenes of trees.

BLUE *picks up a Tote ticket.*

Fifth race. Horse number four. Fifty p. stake.

PEARCE. Diomed Stakes. Won by Gunner B, twelve to one. Wait a moment. Gunner B was horse number four.

BLUE. Well.

PEARCE. Well.

PEARCE. That's six pounds fifty to you.

BLUE. Buy the Mrs. a Kermit Frog.

They go off.

MARGARET *and the* GHOST *of Emily Davison come on.*
MARGARET *walks with her arms folded.*

GHOST. You dozy bitch.

MARGARET. We had a good day out.

GHOST. Family cow.

MARGARET. Bobby only hit Sharon a couple of times —
Sharon only piddled her bed once in the night —

GHOST. And that is success?

MARGARET. That is success.

GHOST. Big deal.

MARGARET. And we backed the winner of The Derby.

GHOST. Stupid, crass dozy bitch of a family cow. Is it me who's
dead or you?

MARGARET. What do you want me to do? Scream?

MARGARET *screams. A silence.*

I do see it. In between worrying that the kids' shoes are too
small. That oranges are too dear. I do see it. As the Nappisan
gurgles down the sink. A good life. Freedom. Being whole.

GHOST. I saw it too, for a second, before the man and the
horse hit me.

The GHOST *and* MARGARET *embrace. Then the* GHOST
*walks away. She remains on the Downs until the end of the
play.*

MARGARET. When I'm tired out, sometimes I think — the real
me — is sulking just behind my shoulder. I could turn, and
look at her, and smile.

SANDY *comes on.*

SANDY. Maggy! Maggy!

MARGARET *and* SANDY *see each other.*

MARGARET. Thought you were with Grandpa. I don't like leaving him alone with the kids.

SANDY. They're all right. Bobby's fleecing the old man at snakes and ladders. One p. a snake.

MARGARET. Where did you put the money?

SANDY. In the dormobile. In the front seat. Where we put the hash once, going over the Turkistan border. Remember?

MARGARET. Before we had kids.

SANDY. Before we had kids.

MARGARET. I remember.

SANDY. Hey.

MARGARET. What?

> SANDY *takes hold of her hands.*

One thousand nine hundred and twenty pounds.

SANDY. Lester Piggott, five to one. That little bookie from the sticks I put it on with. Writhe? I had to wait nearly an hour , while he called in all the money he'd laid off on me. God bless you, Lester! Wherever you are. Sipping your half glass of champagne, chewing your Ryvita biscuit.

MARGARET. It doesn't mean anything, Sandy. The money.

SANDY. Not as much as we'ld have got ante post —

MARGARET. It doesn't mean anything.

SANDY. Means a house. Just.

MARGARET. A house doesn't mean anything.

SANDY. What does then FOR FUCK'S SAKE?

> *For a time they do not look at each other.*

MARGARET. It's all right.

SANDY. Yeah.

MARGARET. Everything is all right.

SANDY. Yeah. Here. We will tell our grandchildren — about the day we backed everything we had in our life — on the winner of The Derby.

MARGARET. Will we?

They go off. The GHOST *walks across the Downs.*
LUNATICS *appear with sacks, picking up the litter.*

1ST LUNATIC. They going to give us a cup of tea, when we've cleared this lot up?

2ND LUNATIC. It's a special treat.

1ST LUNATIC. Should bloody well hope they'ld give us a cup of tea.

3RD LUNATIC. Lester Piggott. Piggott.

2ND LUNATIC. It's a special treat, but your shoes get wet.

4TH LUNATIC. Grassy knoll. Loll on the grassy knoll.

3RD LUNATIC. Piggott.

1ST LUNATIC. In the sack, they said. Then they'ld give us a cup of tea.

2ND LUNATIC. Terrible to tie up, wet laces.

1ST LUNATIC. Got to squeeze the tea-leaves, though.

4TH LUNATIC. On the knoll.

3RD LUNATIC. Piggott.

2ND LUNATIC. And wet socks, terrible.

3RD LUNATIC. Piggott.

4TH LUNATIC. Loll.

A sunset begins to flare. The lights go down.

Methuen's Modern Plays

authors published in the Methuen Modern Plays series are

If you would like to receive, free of charge, regular information about new plays and theatre books from Methuen, please send your name and address to:

The Marketing Department (Drama)
Methuen London Ltd
North Way
Andover
Hampshire SP10 5BE